Wilderness Living

Gregory J. Davenport

STACKPOLE
BOOKS

To my friends, those who take me for what I am

Published by
STACKPOLE BOOKS
5067 Ritter Road
Mechanicsburg, PA 17055
www.stackpolebooks.com

Printed in the United States of America

Cover design by Caroline Stover
Cover and interior illustrations by Steven A. Davenport

10 9 8 7 6 5

First edition

Library of Congress Cataloging-in-Publication Data

Davenport, Gregory J.
    Wilderness living / Gregory J. Davenport. — 1st ed.
        p. cm.
    Includes index.
    ISBN 0-8117-2993-1
    1. Wilderness survival.   2. Outdoor life.   I. Title.

GV200.5 .D38 2001
613.6'9 — dc21

                                                                00-054925

    ISBN 978-0-8117-2993-2

Contents

iv   Contents

Introduction

When I was a kid I watched the television show *Grizzly Adams* and fantasized about living such a life. I had no concept of the harshness wilderness living would bestow upon someone. It isn't that easy. In TV land the cast and crew go home every night. Home—where the food comes from the refrigerator, water from a faucet, heat from a thermostat, and stress reduction from a TV. In a wilderness-living scenario, food and water procurement are a daily struggle, heat will require gathering wood at regular intervals, and the luxuries in life will require using a little ingenuity. There isn't much time for sitting on the couch and watching *Jeopardy*.

If, like me, you desire to live closer to nature, then you'll need to know a few basic and advanced skills to stay alive. *Wilderness Living* is a comprehensive guide that will help you develop these skills and ultimately prepare you for a closer existence with nature.

1
Wilderness Survival

Are you ready for the challenge?

> *The theme of this book is not the fundamentals of survival but rather long-term wilderness living. I felt, however, a short section on the art of global survival skills was needed to round it out.*

Wilderness survival has many variables that dictate a person's success or failure. Each environment presents a myriad of challenges unique to it. Most travelers don't consider this as they venture into several different climates each year. Many have attended *survival schools* that taught them climate specific skills as opposed to solid global principles. In fact, each year more and more of these schools open and most are geared toward desert or aboriginal skills. It is becoming difficult to find schools with seasoned professionals who understand global survival skills (temperate, desert, jungle, arctic/snow). As a global survival professional and owner of Simply Survival (a wilderness education program), I believe in teaching survival principles that can be applied in any environment. If a class is done in a winter/arctic environment we teach the same principles as for one run in the desert. Of course there are specifics that are taught that relate to that particular climate. After years of doing this I have broken the basics of survival into a simple three-step approach that can be applied to any of the various global environments. The following is a *brief* outline of my approach to wilderness survival. For more details on this subject, read my book titled *Wilderness Survival.*

THE THREE-STEP APPROACH TO WILDERNESS SURVIVAL
1. Stop and recognize the situation for what it is.
2. Identify your *five survival essentials* and prioritize them, in order of importance, for the environment that you are in.

1

- Personal Protection (clothing, shelter, fire).
- Signaling (man-made and improvised).
- Sustenance (water/food ID and procurement).
- Travel (with or without a map and compass).
- Health (mental, traumatic, and environmental injuries).

3. Improvise to meet your needs using both your man-made and natural resources.

The following is a more detailed explanation of the three-step approach to wilderness survival:

STOP AND RECOGNIZE THE SITUATION FOR WHAT IT IS

Often, when you realize you are in a legitimate survival situation you panic and begin to wonder aimlessly. This makes it harder for Search and Rescue to find you and valuable time is lost that could have been spent meeting your needs. If you STOP and deal with the situation—evaluating your dilemma and taking appropriate steps—your odds of survival are greatly increased.

IDENTIFY YOUR *FIVE SURVIVAL ESSENTIALS*
AND PRIORITIZE THEM, IN ORDER OF IMPORTANCE,
FOR THE ENVIRONMENT THAT YOU ARE IN

The exact order and method of meeting these needs will depend on the environment you are in. In an arctic climate, shelter may take on a higher priority than it would in a temperate environment during the warm summer months. In the Arctic you may elect to construct a snow cave whereas in the temperate forest you may build a lean-to. Regardless of the order or method you choose, these needs must be met.

The *five survival essentials* are:

Personal Protection (Clothing, Shelter, Fire)

Clothing is your first line of personal protection, shelter your second, and fire the third. So often people will jump to the third line without taking care of the first two. This can prove to be a major error.

- Clothing. For clothes to be effective they should be worn using the COLDER acronym:

C—Keep them CLEAN.

O—Avoid OVERHEATING.

L—Wear them LOOSE and LAYERED. The inner layer wicks the moisture away. (Polyprophylene is a good example of this. Do not use cotton since it loses almost all of its insulating quality when wet.) The middle layer insulates (wool and fleece are two good examples of this). The outer layer protects you from the wind and rain (Gore-Tex is an example of a good outer layer).

D—Keep DRY.

E—EXAMINE clothes daily for damage.

R—REPAIR as deemed necessary.

• Shelter—your second line of personal protection—is so often overlooked. It can make the difference between a cold night out or a warm one. The ability to provide a proper shelter, under adverse conditions, is an extremely important skill for all backcountry travelers to learn. When it's 80 below zero you'll appreciate the comfort of a cozy 30-degree snow cave. On the flip side, when it's 120 degrees a shade shelter will be a pleasant relief from the scorching sun. In addition, a shelter provides a sense of well-being and may help you maintain your will to survive.

Jeff Martin demonstrates the basics of constructing a natural shelter.

Dawn-Marie North emerges from a thermalized A-frame.

The type of shelter you build will depend on the environment, available materials, and time. You should use the following criteria to help with your shelter site selection.

— Large enough for both you and your equipment.
— Close to your construction materials, signaling and recovery site, and food and water sources.
— Located away from potential safety hazards.

Once an appropriate site has been established your shelter construction needs to meet some very basic requirements:

— Use 45- to 60-degree angles on the roofs.
— Shingle all roofing material from bottom to top.
— Vent enclosed shelters.
— Thermalized shelters need at least 8 inches of roofing material.
— In snow shelters, don't let the temperature rise above 32 degrees F.

• Fire is the third line of personal protection. If you have a good shelter that protects you from the elements, a fire may not even be needed. It does, however, provide good light and can be used for many improvising tasks.

For a fire to light and continue to burn it must have all three elements of the fire triangle present. The fire triangle is heat, oxygen, and fuel. If any one of the three is not present, the fire will fail.

— Fuel can be separated into three categories, each building upon the previous one. The three categories of fuel are tinder (anything that will light from a spark), kindling (anything that will light from a small flame), and fuel (anything that will sustain the fire).

— Oxygen is necessary for the fuel to burn and it needs to be present at all stages of a fire. To ensure this happens you'll need a platform and brace. A platform is any dry material that protects your fuel from the ground. A brace is usually a wrist diameter branch that allows oxygen to circulate through the fuel when the fuel is leaned against it.

— Heat is required to start the fire. Since matches and lighters often fail and will eventually run out, you must consider alternative sources of heat to start your fire. Other options include spark-(metal match and flint and steel) and friction-(hand drill, bow and drill, pump drill, fire plow, bamboo fire saw, and fire thong) based heat sources. All are covered in chapter 5.

When building a fire it is important to gather enough fuel to build three knee-high fires. This allows you to go back to a previous stage if the fire starts to die and to keep the fire going while you get more wood. Once the wood is gathered, break it down from big to small—always preparing the smallest stages last. This will help decrease the amount of moisture your tinder and kindling collect during the preparation process. Be sure to gather a platform and brace and use the brace to keep your various stages of fuel off the ground while breaking it down.

Once all the stages are prepared, either light or place the lit tinder on the platform next to the brace. Use the brace to lay your smaller kindling directly over the flame—don't one stick it! In other words, spread a handful of kindling over the flame all at once instead of one stick at a time. Once the flames wick up through the kindling, place another handful across the first. When this stage is going well, advance to the next size. Continue this crisscrossing process until your fuel is burning and the fire is self-supporting. If you have leftover material, it should be set aside—in a dry place—so that it can be used to start another fire later. If you have a problem building your fire, reevaluate your heat, oxygen, and fuel to determine which one is not present or is inadequate for success.

Signaling (Man-Made and Improvised)

A properly utilized signal increases a survivor's chance of affecting his/her own rescue and of ultimately being found. Know how to use your signals prior to needing them. Various man-made and improvised signals are listed here.

• Man-made signals include cellular phones/electronic signals, illumination and smoke flares, commercial signal mirrors, space blankets, and a whistle.

• Improvised signals include fire and smoke, improvised signal mirrors, and ground to air pattern signals.

Students learn how to properly use a signal mirror.

A smoke generator has many benefits as a signaling device.

Sustenance (Water/Food ID and Procurement)

• Water. A survivor can live a month or longer without food but will perish in only 3 to 5 days without water. Under normal conditions the body needs between 2 and 3 quarts per day but in extremely hot/cold conditions or during excessive activity 4 to 6 quarts are necessary. The most common ways of procuring water are: surface, precipitation, subsurface, solar stills, vegetation bag, and transpiration bag.

When procuring water from Mother Nature it is important to purify it in order to destroy those little bugs that can make you so sick. To do this, either boil it for 10 minutes or use iodine tablets (two tablets/quart), bleach drops (two drops/quart), or a commercial device. Once it has been procured and prepared, be sure to protect the water from evaporation or freezing by storing it properly. Contrary to popular belief, avoid blood, seawater, and urine. All will do more to upset your fluid balance than add to it.

• Food. Most backcountry travelers place a high priority on food but in reality it plays a very small role for a survivor. Other priorities such as personal protection, health, or signaling take on a much greater importance. Food does, however, provide the body with valuable nutrients that are lost throughout each day. In addition, its effect on a survivor's morale and attitude cannot be understated. Food can be found from plants, bugs, mollusks, reptiles, fish, birds, and mammals. Various methods of food procurement are covered throughout this book.

Travel (with a Map and Compass)
In almost all survival situations you are better off staying put until a rescue team finds you (be sure to put out a good signal). Three things must be present before you even consider traveling.
• The area you are in does not meet your needs.
• Rescue doesn't appear imminent.
• You know where you are (or can figure it out) and have the skills necessary to travel successfully from point A to point B.

Navigation is an important wilderness skill.

If these criteria are met, then I'd suggest navigating to the nearest well-traveled road. If you have (you should) a map and compass (and know how to use them), they will prove to be valuable tools in accomplishing this task. If not, refer to my chapter on primitive navigation techniques.

At Simply Survival, I teach my students to look at their map before venturing into the wilderness and to establish an emergency heading—from their route of travel—to the nearest well-traveled road. This heading allows them to reach that road no matter where they might be in their trip. By doing this they become aware of the land features around them, and should their situation dictate they walk out, they know which direction to go.

If you decide to travel, make sure to leave a note that lists the time you left, the route you intend to travel, and your intended destination. In addition, mark your trail by tying flags to branches, breaking branches, etc.

Health (Mental, Traumatic, and Environmental Injuries)

• Mental. I believe that your will to survive plays a major role in your ability to overcome what seem like insurmountable odds. Why do people perish in a warm temperate environment while others thrive in a hot desert or cold arctic region? Circumstances or will? Perhaps it is their mental attitude that makes the difference. Perhaps they had something that motivated them to stay alive. Perhaps it was their faith or maybe it was their family. Perhaps it was that their spouse had the checkbook. No matter what it was, they harnessed that energy to create a positive framework and motivation to stay alive. You will need to do the same. Don't just sit down and feel sorry for yourself.

• Traumatic injuries should be attended to as soon as possible. Use basic first aid skills to deal with any trauma that might occur. Protect your airway, stop bleeding, prevent shock, and immobilize all potential fractures. Before departing to the far ends of the earth, attend a good basic first aid class or a prehospital emergency care program.

• Environmental injuries must be prevented. Once they occur, your logical mind will start to wander and you'll begin making mistakes that could mean the difference between life and death. To avoid heat and cold injuries, protect yourself from the environment by using proper *personal protection* techniques that were discussed earlier. In addition to the climate, you also need to be conscious of what poisonous plants, insects, and snakes are in the area and prepare to deal with any potential problems related to them. Do your research!

IMPROVISE TO MEET YOUR NEEDS USING BOTH YOUR MAN-MADE AND NATURAL RESOURCES

Stop, recognize your five survival essentials, prioritize them in order of preference for the environment and situation you're in, and improvise to meet those needs. I believe that this process is the key to survival. The only thing that changes from one environment to the next is the order in which you meet your needs and the methods you use to meet them. Sometimes the answer is straightforward and sometimes it isn't.

When I need some help deciding how to best meet one of my needs I use the *five steps of improvising* approach.

1. Determine your need.
2. Inventory your available materials.
   - Man-made
   - Natural
3. Consider the different options of how you might meet your need.
4. Pick one based on its efficient use of the following:
   - Time
   - Energy
   - Materials
5. Proceed with the plan. Ensure the final product is safe and durable.

Wilderness survival is a logical process. I realize there are situations that may dictate success or failure. Perhaps you wreck your car causing an open fracture of your femur and find you're pinned in place by the steering wheel. To make matters worse you are on an old abandoned logging road 50 miles from civilization, your vehicle is leaking gas, and there's a forest fire rapidly approaching your area. In situations like these there is no clear-cut answer on how to proceed. For snow skiers or backpackers, however, who find themselves in a survival scenario, using a logical step-by-step approach will help them keep a clear head and proceed with meeting their needs even under the most adverse conditions.

2

Buckskin

Wearing his wool jacket, the hunter takes his game. He quickly skins it, cuts it into quarters, and is happy he has replenished his food cache. He often leaves the hide without consideration for his future clothing needs.

> *The first time I tanned a hide, the process seemed never-ending. It had been easy to make tools and blood sausage from the animal, and the meat had tasted really good. The cold that made the robe necessary, however, also hampered my attempts at making the hide useful. Before I was finished, my hands were cracked and bleeding and the hide's white streaks were evidence of the poor job I had done. I wondered how long it would take before I could make a good piece of buckskin—after all there were no clothing stores around the corner.*

PREPARING A HIDE

SKINNING AN ANIMAL
Before skinning an animal, be sure it is dead. Once you're sure, cut the animal's throat and collect the blood in a container for later use. If time is not an issue, wait 30 minutes before starting to skin. This allows the body to cool, which in turn makes it easier to skin and also provides enough time for most parasites to leave the animal's hide.

Small Game
Glove skinning is the method most often used for skinning small game. Hang the animal from its hind legs and make a circular cut just above the leg joints. Don't cut through the tendon! To avoid dulling your knife (occurs when cutting from the fur side), slide a finger between the hide and muscle

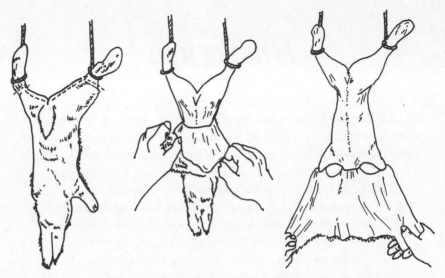

Glove skinning small game.

Students learn how to skin small game.

and place your knife next to the muscle so that you cut the hide from the nonhair side. Cut down the inside of each leg, ending close to the genital area, and peel the skin off the legs until you reach the animal's tail. Firmly slide a finger under the hide between the tail and spine until you have a space that allows you to cut the tail free. Do the same on the front side. At this point the hide can be pulled down and free from the animal's membrane with little effort. Avoid squeezing the belly since this may cause urine to spill onto the meat. Pull the front feet through (inside out) the hide by sliding a finger between the elbow and the membrane and pulling the leg up and free from the rest of the hide. Cut off the feet. The head can be either severed or skinned depending on your talents.

For very small game one-cut skinning can be done by making a cut along the animal's back and pulling the hide, at the cut, in opposite directions until removed. This method destroys most of the hide and should only be used on the smallest of animals.

Large Game
A larger animal can be hung from a tree by its hind legs or skinned while lying on the ground. To hang it by its hind legs, find the tendon that connects the upper and lower leg and poke a hole between it and the bone. If musk glands are present, remove them. (Musk glands are usually found at the bend between the upper and lower parts of the hind legs.) Free the hide from the animal's genitals by cutting a circular area around them, and then make an incision that runs just under its hide and all the way up to the neck. To avoid cutting the entrails, slide your index and middle fingers between the hide and the thin membrane enclosing the entrails. Use the V between the fingers to guide the cut and push the entrails down and away from the knife. The knife should be held with its back side next to the membrane and the sharp side facing out so that when used it cuts the hide from the nonhair side. Next, cut around the joint of each extremity. From there, extend the cut down the inside of each leg until it reaches the midline incision.

You should attempt to pull off the hide using the same method as done for small game. If you end up needing to use your knife, be sure to cut toward the meat so as not to damage the hide (avoid cutting through the entrails or the hide). If skinning on the ground, use the hide to protect the meat and don't remove it until after you gut and butcher the animal. Once

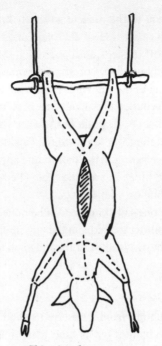

Skinning large game.

the hide has been removed it can be tanned and used for many different needs such as clothing, shelter cover, containers, etc.

Sinew

On larger animals, be sure to salvage the sinew that can be found along their backbone and the tendon that runs on the back side of the lower hind legs. Sinew has many uses in the improvising process—from clothing to weaponry. For further details, refer to the end of this chapter.

The Animal's Brain

Almost all animals have enough brains to tan their own hide. The easiest way to remove an animal's brain is to make a V-shaped cut—with a hacksaw—into its skull (antlers in the middle). If a hacksaw is not available, simply smash the skull with a stone, being careful not to cut yourself on the bones' sharp edges. Once the brain is exposed, remove it and store it until ready for use.

Other Useful Parts

Other than food, hide, and sinew, an animal can provide many useful parts that can be used for improvising. Blood sausage from the intestines, weapons from bones, glue from the hide, and hammers from bones are just a few examples. Try to use as much of the animal as you can—the only limiting factor is your imagination.

TANNING A HIDE

A hide can meet many of your needs and care should be taken to use as much of it as you can. Since your final product is affected by how well you skin the hide, take care to avoid damaging it during the process.

TANNING MATERIALS

• Scraping beam: I prefer to use a large waist beam for scraping an animal's hide. The ideal pole will be 5 to 7 feet long (length = your height), 6 to 8 inches in diameter, well rounded, and with a smooth working surface. Stabilize the beam so that the up end is waist high. This will allow you to scrape the hide in a pushing motion while leaning against the pole. (The hide should hang slightly over the top of the pole so that you can hold it in place when you lean against it.)

• Scraper: an ideal scraper will be straight and have a defined edge (not a sharp cutting edge—just a distinct one). Bones are the most commonly used primitive scraping tools.

A waist beam provides the necessary support needed when preparing a hide to be tanned.

A bone can be used to scrape the flesh from the animal's hide.

- Two to three gallons of hardwood ash: a lye solution made from ash and water is used to soak the hide.
- Five-gallon container to mix the ash in.
- Dressing: brains and egg yolks are the dressings most often used to help soften a hide. Other less often used options are spinal cords, milk, rotten fir or oak wood, soaproot and yucca root, acorn soup (not leached), saguaro seeds, and jojoba seeds.
- Wringing stick: a strong 3- to 4-foot stick.
- Softening tool: a length of cable or rope tied to the top and bottom of a tree can be used to help stretch and soften a hide. Pumice (light, porous volcanic rock) can be used to help abrade the hide. (If the pumice makes cuts into the hide—replace it with another.)
- Glue: used to produce a sack from the hide. Elmer's, wood, and hide glue (covered later) are all options.

THE PROCESS OF TANNING A HIDE (HAIR OFF)

Fleshing
Fleshing is the process of removing all the meat, fat, and large membrane from the animal's hide. To accomplish this, lay the hide over your waist beam (flesh side up) allowing a small amount to drape over the top of the pole. Press your abdomen against the top of the pole and the hide—applying enough pressure to hold the hide in place. Use a scraping tool to remove meat, fat, and membrane by pushing it down into the hide, forward, and off. Continue until the whole hide is done, always moving from a fleshed area

to one that isn't. Focus on the meat and fat for now and don't be overzealous during this stage. There will be better opportunities to remove the membrane later.

Soaking

A lot of people soak their hides in fresh water, which requires them to change it at least two times a day and to speculate wildly on when it has soaked enough. Soaking a hide in an alkali solution (lye water) will help alleviate these problems.

To create this alkali solution, mix approximately 2 gallons of hardwood white ash to 1 gallon of water (2:1 ratio) and stir it together with a stick. Be sure to use a wooden barrel, plastic bucket, or stainless steel container and stir it with a wooden stick. Do not use aluminum or tin containers since they are badly corroded by the caustic solution. Let sit for several hours and then pour the solution through a porous cloth into another container. (Since lye can and will burn you, be sure to wear rubber gloves, eye protection, and an apron when working with it.) To determine if the mixture is right, place an egg or small potato in the solution (make sure it has enough room to float in the liquid—even if you have to lean the bucket to one side). If it sinks, the solution is too weak; if it floats and turns sideways, it is too strong. When the mixture is just right, the egg will float so that approximately ½ to 1 inch of its top is showing above the surface. If the egg sinks, you can boil down the lye water—making it stronger—until it supports the egg correctly. If the egg turns sideways, you can add water (1 cup at a time)—making it weaker—until it supports the egg correctly. CAUTION: THIS SOLUTION CAN AND WILL BURN YOUR SKIN AND YOUR EYES AND IS HARMFUL IF SWALLOWED. THE CONTAINER SHOULD BE COVERED, MARKED, AND KEPT OUT OF ANIMALS' AND CHILDREN'S REACH. If any of the lye solution gets on your skin, wash it off with vinegar. If it gets in your eyes, you need to rinse thoroughly for 20 minutes and seek immediate medical attention. Make sure you move the hide around until you are certain that it is completely covered by the solution. At this point, I like to place a weight on top of the hide—to ensure that it stays below the solution's surface—and cover the container with a lid. How long to soak the hide depends on many factors (weather conditions, thickness of the hide, and so on). As a general rule, however, 3 to 5 days should be adequate (10 days is considered the maximum amount of time when using an alkali solution). When you take the hide out of the bucket, thoroughly rinse off all of the ash solution before moving on to the next step.

Graining

Graining is similar to the fleshing process. Your goal here is to remove hair, epidermis, and the hide's underlying grain. If the grain is not removed, it will be more difficult to soften that area of the hide. To accomplish this, lay your hide on the waist beam with its hair running downward. Leaning up against the beam and securing the hide with your waist, begin scraping

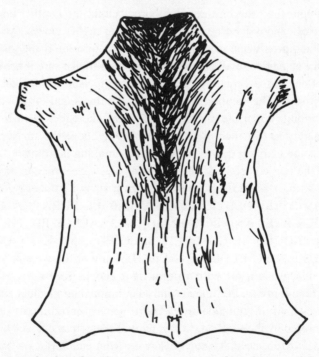

The upper back and neck are harder to grain than the rest of the hide.

at the midback. Save the harder neck and upper back until you are warmed up and have developed a good stroke. Each scraping stroke should begin above its intended area using a firm downward and continuous stroke that runs approximately 1 to 2 inches. The key is to be fairly aggressive and to stop prior to pushing the stroke over the grain (even if you have to take extremely short strokes). If you find your stroke is only removing hair and not the grain, readjust and take shorter hard-driving strokes. Rescrape the area several times to make sure the grain is removed. Always move from a scraped section to an unscraped section in a very systematic pattern. When advancing to another section, be sure the first is completely done and allow for an overlapping stroke between the two. When you get around to the upper back and neck it's best to scrape up the neck and then sideways. This area will be very difficult to do and may require you to take shorter and harder strokes.

Hide scars pose a problem since they are prone to tearing during this process. In most cases you'll need to either let them tear or accept that a little grain cannot be removed. When scraping a hole, scrape toward its center—from all angles—instead of across its surface (which tends to extend the hole's size). Once the grain is removed, the hide will have a dull rough appearance; any grain left will look shiny, smooth, and slightly raised.

Membraning

Membraning is the process of removing the membrane tissue left on the flesh side of the hide (use the same technique as with graining). If you let the hide dry out after graining (a common practice), soak it until it becomes workable. The membrane may not appear to have a clearly defined end to it but as long as you work in a systematic pattern most of it will be either removed or at least broken down.

At this point the hide needs to be rinsed. This can be done in a creek, river, lake, or by placing a hose inside a large bucket. Rinsing is complete when the hide is soft and flexible (usually 12 or more hours). Once done you need to wring all of the moisture from the hide. In order for the dressing process to be successful, it is very important to get rid of the hide's moisture. Use any mechanical advantage you can to accomplish this. Wringing sticks work great.

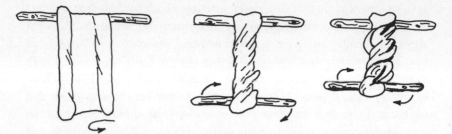

Use any mechanical advantage you can to get the moisture out of the hide.

Dressing

Dressings help condition and soften a hide. Mix 1 pound of brains (or 12 egg yokes) with ½ gallon of lukewarm water. (As a general rule it takes about 1 pound of brains or 1 dozen beaten egg yokes to tan a deer hide.) Place the *well wrung* hide into the solution and move it around until its whole surface has been saturated. To ensure it is completely covered, pull out all of the hide's wrinkles. Soak the hide for a minimum of ½ hour—longer if you'd like. Once you are sure it has absorbed the dressing, take it out and stretch out any wrinkles. If you find an area that has a fair amount of resistance—finish stretching it and then put it back into the dressing for another 5 minutes.

At this point the hide is ready to soften. If you aren't ready to soften the hide, however, refrigerate or dry it. If you dry it, you'll need to soak it for several hours before it's ready to soften. Be sure to wring out as much moisture from the hide as a mechanical advantage will allow before beginning the softening process.

Softening

To prevent the hide's fibers from locking together, you'll need to work it while it transforms from wet to dry. To keep the hide from becoming hard, it is important to avoid any long time gaps in this process—especially after much moisture has been removed. Don't forget to work both sides. Hand softening and frame softening are the two most common techniques used during this process.

Hand Softening

Begin by stretching the hide from neck to tail and then side to side. Using a systematic approach will help you cover its entire surface. You may elect to drape the hide over your knees or perhaps hang it from a pole during this process. Or perhaps you have a thin cable (braided rawhide is another option) that can be used to both stretch and abrade the hide. A cable can be loosely secured to the bottom of a tree and again at about 7 feet up. To stretch a hide with the cable, fold the hide over it (don't bunch it up) and work it back and forth in a pulling action. Once the initial stretch is done, focus on the hide's perimeter. This area is thin and will dry fast and should be done early on. For optimal results, the outer edge is pulled between the thumb and fingers until the hand slides off the hide.

If available, use a cable to help soften the hide.

The whole process may take several hours to complete. You'll know you're almost done when the hide becomes dry, white, and stretchy. At that point you'll need to abrade it (stretch it out and aggressively rub an abrading tool across its surface) until all the crust is gone and it takes on a buffed appearance. Be sure to do both sides. Pumice, mussel shells, and aged bone sponge (from the ball of a large animal's humerus) are excellent abraders.

Frame Softening

Lashing four poles together and tying the hide tightly within its inner opening provides an excellent structure for working the hide while it dries. The size of your frame will depend on the size of the hide you are softening. Make cuts ¼ inch in from the hide's edge (they should be parallel to the edge) and secure it to the frame with leather thongs. For best results use four lines and tie the hide as shown in the illustration that follows. Try to provide even tension across the whole hide. If you don't have a softening stick— a straight, round, 2-inch-wide piece of wood with a slightly rounded beveled tip on one end—you'll need one.

Using the softening stick, aggressively work the hide (be careful around holes) by stroking it—with the stick—while leaning in with your whole

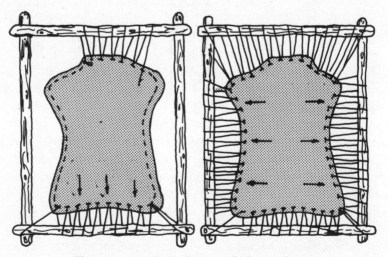

The proper method of tying a hide to a frame.

body. After an initial stretching, focus on the edges in the same fashion as done when hand softening. As the hide stretches, it may be necessary to tighten the lines around its supporting framework. The whole process may take several hours to complete. You'll know you're almost done when the hide becomes dry, white, and stretchy. At that point you'll need to abrade it until all the crust is gone and it takes on a buffed appearance. Be sure to do both sides. Pumice, mussel shells, and aged bone sponge (from the ball of a large animal's humerus) are excellent abraders.

Smoking

Smoking is necessary to create a hide that will remain soft even after it is washed. To do this you'll need to create a smoking pit and make the hide into a sack.

• Smoking pit. Start by digging a 2-foot pit that is no wider than the neck opening of the hide(s) you are smoking. Be sure to clear the area around your hole of all flammable materials. Other options are to use a smudge pot or a woodstove.

• Turning the hide into a sack. Either glue or sew two hides together to make a sack (grain side in). If you only have one, then fold it lengthwise on itself. Either way, seal the hide from the tail end to the neck corners— leaving the neck region open. If using glue, use a very thin line and avoid letting it contact other areas of the hide's surface. To keep the hide clean, make a skirt (cylinder of same diameter as the neck opening) from cotton or wool and attach it to the hide opening.

To suspend the hide above the smoker hole use either a tripod or a pole placed between two bipods. Use scrap leather strips to secure it to the supporting poles so that it is void of wrinkles and hangs freely. Make sure there are no folds and that the inner sides are not touching each other. To do this, it may be necessary to use thin dry sticks to prop open the hide. If using sticks, be sure to move them often so that the whole hide gets smoked. Start a fire close—but not too close—to your smoker and let it establish a good bed of coals. I prefer to use a hardwood for this. Move the coals to the bottom of your smoker and cover them completely with punk (decayed wood). You'll need approximately 5 gallons of punk wood (be sure the punk wood doesn't contain any pitch since it will easily flame up). Next, position the hide over the hole so that the skirt can be secured to the ground with a

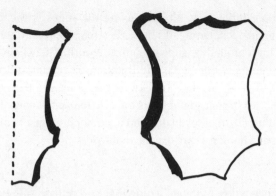

When preparing the hide for smoking, either attach two hides together or fold one hide in half.

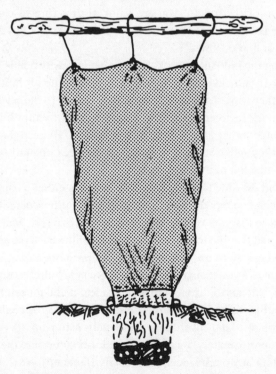

When smoking a hide, make sure there are no folds and that the inner sides are not touching each other.

A nice tanned elk hide.

couple of baseball-size rocks (completely enclosing the pit). The smoking process will take anywhere from ½ hour to several hours to complete. At regular intervals (about every 3 to 5 minutes), slightly raise the skirt to check the smoker's heat level, adding punk wood when needed. If at anytime it flames up, move the hide to the side and add more punk wood until the flames subside. Although it is not necessary to smoke the flesh side, many people do. Simply turning the hide inside out and repeating the above accomplishes this. The longer you smoke the hide the darker in color it will be.

Once you have finished tanning the hide it becomes a dynamic material for use in many different improvised items—from clothes (shirts, pants, shoes, headgear) to a holding pouch, to a shelter covering. The uses are unlimited.

THE PROCESS OF TANNING A HIDE (HAIR ON)

A hide with the hair on is useful as a robe, blanket, or mat. Tanning a hide without removing the hair is slightly different than when the hair is removed. Attention needs to be given to not damaging the hair side of the hide. Once the hide has been removed from the animal it should be tied within your lashed frame (explained in preceding section under softening) as soon as possible.

Fleshing/Membraning

Make sure to get even pressure across the whole hide. Using a fleshing tool, remove the hide's flesh, fat, and membrane with an overhead stabbing/downward type motion. A fleshing tool can be made from bone, wood, or by lashing a mussel shell to a handle. It should be sharp but not so sharp that it can cut or damage the hide. Bones prove to be the perfect choice since it is unlikely you'll ever get them too sharp to damage the skin. If you are unable to move on to the next step (dressing), dry the hide. If you do dry it, be sure to briefly soak it in fresh water before proceeding.

Dressing

Remove the hide from the frame and place it into the dressing solution. Work it around to make sure it gets completely covered. Let it soak in the dressing overnight. Remove the hide and rinse the hair side well before wringing out as much moisture as you can. Do not use any mechanical advantage in this process since it may damage the hair side.

Frame Softening

Using the softening stick, aggressively work the hide (be careful around holes) by stroking it with the stick in the same manner as previously mentioned. However, only work the flesh side of the hide.

Smoking

To smoke the hide, it will need to be prepared in the same way as previously mentioned. You only need to smoke the flesh side, however.

CLEANING A TANNED HIDE

Cleaning a tanned hide isn't much different than having a delicate shirt that requires special attention when washed. If washed in hot water or dried with excessive heat, it will shrink and may become stiff. Therefore, simply use cold or warm water, hand wash with a mild soap, and line dry. It may be a little stiff when done but this will loosen up after you put it on and move around in it.

MAKING RAWHIDE

Rawhide is good leather for improvising tools and equipment. It is not, however, preferred for clothing. It is easy to make. Start by soaking the hide in lye solution or water that is changed frequently until the hair literally falls out when lightly rubbed. Flesh the hide as before. Instead of graining the hide, dehair with your fleshing tool by applying just enough downward pressure to remove the hair. Thoroughly rinse it and membrane as usual. Let it dry. The newly created rawhide can be cut into workable sections, soaked in water, and then used in your improvising process. It is a wonderful material for lashing and so on, since it shrinks and hardens when it dries.

SINEW

Sinew is a natural animal material that can be dried and shredded into a very strong string and has often been used as sewing thread and cordage. It is a fibrous tendon that connects bones to muscles and is most commonly procured from the back and lower leg of big game animals like deer, elk, and moose, as well as cattle.

SINEW FROM LEG

Animals like deer have a tendon that runs along the back of the leg from their "knee" to their "ankle." With a knife, cut the area between the tendon and the bone and sever the tendon at its top and bottom. Skin the hide away from the tendon and then with a pair of pliers peel the sinew's outer sheath back and off. The sheath is too hard to use and can be set aside. Let the sinew dry for several days in an area free of sun and insects, and out of animal and rodent reach. I like to turn it daily to speed up the process. Once it is dry, pound the sinew until the fibers begin to separate. To avoid cutting the sinew, take care not to strike it with the hammer's edge. Using your hands (and the hammer again if you need to) pull the fibers apart until they are all the size of small twine. Tie the threads together into bundles of similar length (about fifteen lines per bundle) and set them aside until ready for use.

BACKSTRAP SINEW

The two long silvery bands of backstrap sinew run along both sides of the animal's backbone resting on top of its long back muscles. Peel away any fat that may rest on top of the sinew and then slide a dull knife under it. To lift the sinew free, tilt the back side of the knife up and scrape the full length of its underside to remove any attached meat and fat. Alternate between lifting and scraping as you go. Once you free as much as you can, cut it at both ends (often the shoulder end will come free during the process). Let the sinew dry for several days in an area free of sun, insects, and out of animal and rodent reach. Turn it daily until dry. Backstrap sinew is a lot easier to break down than sinew from the leg and can often be done by simply twisting it between the thumb and index finger of each hand. Another method of breaking down backstrap sinew is to create a comb (made of nails that have been hammered through a board) and drag the sinew across it. Either way, continue the process until the strands are the size of small twine. Tie the threads together into bundles of similar length (about fifteen lines per bundle) and set them aside until ready for use.

3

Improvised Clothing

The market provides us with polypropylene, fleece, and Gore-Tex—exactly what are these materials and how did we dress before they were created?

> *The Arctic was cold and the desert was hot. It was*
> *amazing to learn that the same clothes that kept me*
> *warm in extreme cold also kept me cool during the*
> *hottest of days. To adjust for the various temperatures—*
> *created by both the climate and my workload—I became*
> *a master at adding and removing layers of clothing.*
> *When in the wilderness, I pay close attention to my*
> *clothing—recognizing it as my first line of personal*
> *protection.*

BUCKSKIN CLOTHING

REPAIRING HOLES IN THE HIDE

Once a hide has been tanned it may have a few holes in it related to its original injury or the process itself. It is best to repair these flaws before you use the material to improvise clothing or for other purposes. Since the holes are probably not uniform in size, they should be trimmed.

Sew the hide from the flesh side using sinew, leather, or heavy-duty thread. The two stitches I most often use are a running stitch (only in a pinch) and the locking stitch.

Running Stitch

The running stitch is a continuous stitch from beginning to end. This method's biggest flaw is that if the line breaks at any given point it compromises the whole stitch.

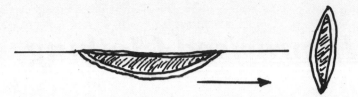

Trim a hole until it has a uniform appearance.

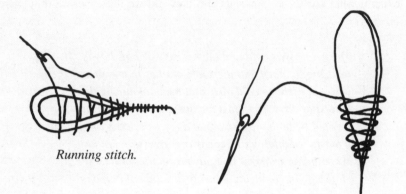

Running stitch.

Locking stitch.

Locking Stitch

A locking stitch is similar to the running stitch except that each time the thread comes through the flesh side it is run back through itself before tightened down. This prevents the line from coming out completely when a section gets worn or breaks.

If you don't have thread, sinew is a good alternative. If you don't have a needle, improvise one from bone or wood.

Improvised Needles

Needles can be made from bone or wood. If bone, you can usually find a shred that is created during the breaking process. The piece can be worked on a rock until it takes on the shape of a needle (the rock will work like sandpaper). On one end the tip should be sharpened to a point and on the other left broad like you'd see with a store-bought needle. Use a flint-knapped tip or awl to create an eye on the wider end of the bone. If using wood, you can create the same result by using your knife or a flint-knapped tip. The size of the needle will depend upon the type of work you intend to do. Since bone needles are generally stronger, they are preferred when working with buckskin.

SELECTING THE RIGHT HIDE

Hide selection will vary depending on what you intend to use it for. When using a hide for clothing you should consider three factors: thickness, texture (stretch), and color. It's best to select material that is similar in all areas.

Thickness

A hide's thickness will vary from animal to animal and as a general rule, a hide from a doe or young buck will be thinner. A thinner hide will be more appropriate for summer wear and a thicker one for winter. Since it's not very often that a piece of clothing can be made from one hide, it's important to use hides of similar thickness when you can. If this is impossible, however, try to balance out the clothing article. For example, if making a shirt, you may decide to use the thicker hides for the chest/back and the thinner pieces for the arms (providing balance). For pants, you may use the thicker material for the upper half and then attach thinner hides to just below the knees (on both sides).

Texture

Texture describes the tightness of the hide's fibers. Hides that are loose fibered tend to stretch and are more malleable. Hides with tight fibers have minimal stretch and appear grainy. For best results, select hides that have similar stretch qualities. Once again, if this is impossible, try to balance the clothing article by appropriate placement of hides with similar texture.

Color

A hide takes on most of its color during the smoking process. Thus it is best to select skins for your clothes prior to smoking.

CUTTING THE BUCKSKIN PATTERN

Before laying out your hide for use, get it damp and stretch it until it is smooth. Evaluate your skin for size, making sure it is large enough for the intended pattern plus a little. In addition, make sure to orient the hide so that its spine runs the length of the pattern's arms, legs, and trunk (versus across these areas). The spine is a dividing line and the hide on both sides is usually of similar thickness. Leave the arms and legs a little long—roll them up until after a few washings and then trim them.

SEWING BUCKSKIN
Sewing your buckskin pattern together is different from repairing a hole. The edges of your buckskin will be far thicker then the tears that you have already repaired.

Sewing Material
Although sinew thread can be used, it is not very practical on clothes that get heavy use and multiple washings. In such a case it tends to fray and eventually break. If you do decide to use it, use fairly thick pieces or braid several smaller ones together. A better option is to sew the seams with buckskin. These long thongs can be created from the previously trimmed edges of your hide. Cut away the excess, creating a long thong like you might find in a store-bought leather shoelace. For best results, use the inner thick part of the trimmed piece, not the natural outer edge, since it tends to be thin. To make it easier for the thong to slide through the hide's hole, cut the working end to a point.

Preparing the Seam
In most cases you will need to use a punch to establish the holes along your seam before you begin sewing. This can be done with a bone awl that has a sharp, tapered point. Begin by laying out your material in the established pattern, making sure that each piece is aligned and comfortable. Using the awl, punch holes in the seams (of both the top and bottom pieces), keeping an equal distance between each hole. The hole's size should be just big enough for the thong to squeak through.

Stitching with a Thong

How to Start a Seam
To begin a thong stitch, create a hole in the end without a tailored point. Run the pointed end down through the first hole, back up through the second

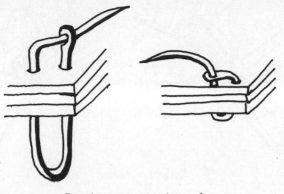

Starting a seam using a thong.

hole, and then through the hole at its other end. The thong is then pulled tight to create a cinched-down start to your seam.

Splicing One Thong to Another

As one thong approaches its end, another will need to be spliced to it. To do this, punch a hole in your second thong and run the pointed end of the first one through it. Next, punch a hole about 1 to 2 inches back from the tip of the first thong and run the pointed end of the second one through it. Go ahead and cut off the excess from the first piece and pull the two tightly together.

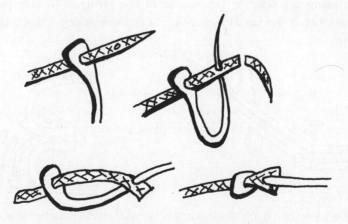

Splicing two pieces of rawhide together.

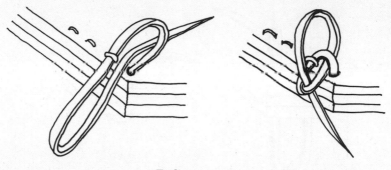

Ending a seam.

Ending the Thong Stitch

Once the thong has gone through the last hole, run it back through the previous stitch on the same side. This will create a loop between the last hole and the previous stitch; run the thong back through this hole. Another loop is created from the previous step and the thong should be run back down through it. Pull each one of these stitches tight and trim the thong.

Using the Thong to Sew a Seam

Most seams can be sewn using a running or locking stitch that is either hidden or exposed. If hidden, the stitch is done with the garment turned inside out; when completed the garment is turned right side out. If exposed, the seams are sewn on the outside of the garment. To help provide a stronger seam that has a lesser chance of breaking, a strip of buckskin (welt)

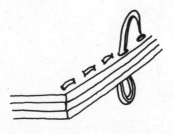 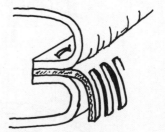

Sewing a seam, on the inside, using a running stitch and placing a welt between the materials.

Sewing a seam, on the outside, using a running stitch.

is often placed between the two pieces being sewn together. In addition, if fringe is desired, it is easy to create from a welt.

BASIC CLOTHING DESIGNS

Breechcloth

The breechcloth is similar to a diaper in that it only covers the buttocks and groin area. Its design is simply a long piece of buckskin that runs between your legs while its two free ends hang over a belt (in front and in back). It is ideal for warm weather but in cooler temperatures you may want to add leggings. Another point to consider is the texture of the hide you use. I'd advise a hide that is fairly soft.

Breechcloth.

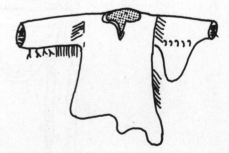

Leggings.

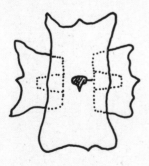

Buckskin shirt.

Leggings (Commonly Used with a Breechcloth)

Leggings cover your legs, not your crotch. The first step in making leggings is to find two hides of similar quality that are big enough to wrap loosely around each leg. Each one will be independent of the other. Simply trim the hide and stitch it up leaving plenty of room and a flap at the top that can be attached to your belt.

Buckskin Shirt

A buckskin shirt is often made from three hides (one for the torso and one for each arm). Cut a hole in the torso section at the point where you want your head to go through and stabilize it with a locking stitch. The arm sections are sewn to the torso piece and then together on the underside. If fringe is desired on the arms, then either use a welt or create it from any excess material that is hanging below the stitch line. Finally, sew the front and back of the torso's sides together.

A buckskin shirt is easy to make.

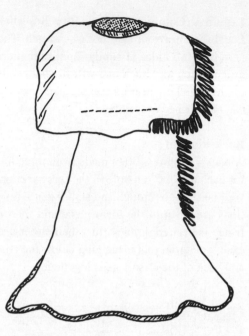

Buckskin dress.

Buckskin Dress

A buckskin dress is simply a shirt that is often made longer by attaching additional hides to the bottom of the upper section.

Buckskin (or Rawhide) Shoes

Buckskin shoes can be very comfortable but will wear out relatively quickly. Thus thicker hides or perhaps even rawhide are preferred for the soles. Cut a pattern similar to the one displayed on the next page and sew the two pieces together. Since there is so much wear on the material, I prefer to sew it with a thong using a locking stitch so that the seam is not in direct contact with the ground.

Immediate Action Shoe

Buckskin can be used to create an immediate action shoe by cutting it into a triangle and wrapping it around your foot. Using several pieces with grass

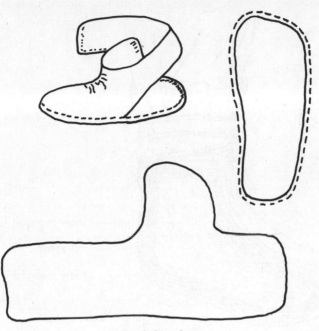

Buckskin shoe.

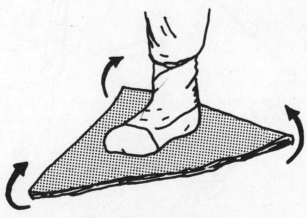

Immediate action shoe.

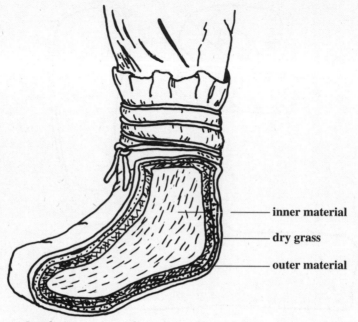

inner material

dry grass

outer material

Insulating an immediate action shoe provides additional warmth.

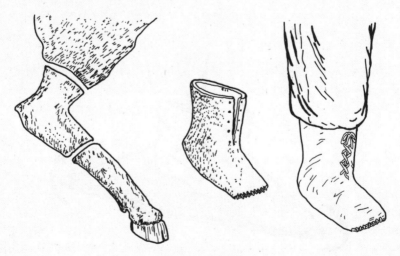

Moose hock shoe.

or similar materials between each layer will provide additional insulation during cold weather. Tying a thong around the top can hold these shoes together.

Moose Hock Shoes

Hock skin is the skin from the lower leg of a deer or similar animal. The hock skin of moose and caribou provides a perfect fit for a shoe. Cut the skin and entire leg above and below the lower joint, separate it from the muscle, and pull it down and over the leg. Take time to remove as much of the flesh as possible from the membrane side of the hock. Cut a slit from the inside top to just above the moose hock's joint and use an awl to punch holes for lacing. Sew shut the bottom opening.

Gaiters

Gaiters are best made from hides with the hair left on. They are easy to make by simply cutting a section of hide large enough to wrap around the part of your leg that extends from just above the ankle to below the knee. Use an awl to punch holes through the two sides of the hide and then lace them together with a thong. To prevent moisture from entering through the laced area, I prefer to place the lacing on the calf side of my leg.

INSULATION

In hot environments clothes keep you cool; in a cold environment those same clothes keep you warm. This principle is based on a theory of insulation: the ability to surround yourself with material that prevents the passage of heat into or out of it. Insulation is produced by trapping dead air between the fibers of each individual garment and between the layers of pieces worn one over another.

In desert regions of the world people wear long flowing robes that cover their whole body. The robe is usually made up of several layers to help protect them from the unyielding heat. In addition, most wear a hat with a neck drape and a dead air space between the top of their head and the hat. Using modern materials, this is easy. If using a hide it is probably best to use a thin hide and to sew your seams loosely together, perhaps even leaving gaps between the materials. Thin hides can be obtained from young bucks or a doe.

In an arctic or snow environment you should use a thicker hide and sew your seams as tight as possible. To increase your clothing insulation, you may decide to add a layer of dry cattail, duff, leaves, or grass between several garments. Hides with the hair left on will also aid in heightened insulative qualities.

In a rainy environment it is best not to use buckskin if other options are available. The hide tends to soak up the moisture and stretch out of shape.

BUTTONS
On some garments you may elect to use buttons instead of lacing with a thong. Buttons can be improvised from buckskin, antlers, bones, shells, or hardwood.

Buckskin Buttons
To create a button from buckskin, cut a triangular piece that is about 6 inches long with a 2-inch-wide base. Starting at the base, roll the buckskin up, leaving 2½ to 3 inches free. Punch a hole through the rolled section and then run your pointed end through it, pulling it tight. Use the excess material to attach the button to your clothing. To use, either attach a thong to the other side of the garment or punch a hole through it. If you do create a buttonhole, make it so that the button barely fits though and be sure to stitch its outer side. Another option is to run a short piece of thong through both sides of the garment and to then tie it off.

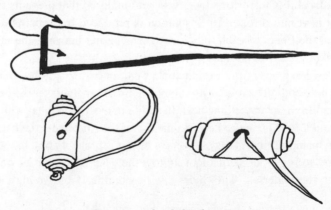

Creating a buckskin button.

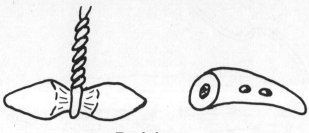

Toggle button.

Toggle Buttons

A toggle button can be made from bone, wood, antler, or any other similar material. Use a piece that is about 1 to 2 inches long and bevel the ends and center so that its two highest points are at the one-third and two-thirds marks of its length. Tie a thong to the center of the toggle and attach it to one side of the garment. As with the buckskin button you can either create a buttonhole or use a thong on the other side. A similar design can be created from an antler tip by grooving the center or creating two buttonholes in it.

Round Buttons

Round buttons can be made from hardwood, antlers, or shells. Hardwood buttons can be created with a knife and awl by simply whittling them into shape and then punching holes with your awl. Shells may provide a readily usable shape. They tend, however, to break when you try to make a hole in them with a punch. Instead of the punch, use a small stone bit with a pump drill (covered in chapter 5) to create your holes. Although antlers provide an excellent material for buttons, they may be hard to use unless you have a hacksaw. If you do have a hacksaw, cut buttons from the wide end of the

Wood, antler, or shell button.

Sun/snow goggles.

antler and drill holes into their center with the awl. As with any button, they can be attached to one side with a thong and you can either use a thong or create a buttonhole on the other side.

SUN/SNOW GOGGLES

In certain environments (usually desert and snow) it is necessary to protect your eyes from the sun's reflection. Sun or snow blindness is a very painful and debilitating condition and not one you want to deal with. To improvise a pair of sun/snow goggles, cut a piece of leather (bark or other pliable material can also be used) that is long and wide enough to cover both of your eyes. Next, make small horizontal slits at the point where the material is directly over each eye. Finally, tie a line to both sides of the goggles that is long enough to be tied in back when the goggles are on.

SLEEPING COVER/BLANKET

A sleeping cover is normally made from a hide that still has its hair. In order to be large enough, you may need to sew several pieces together. For optimal results it is ideal to have one above and below you, but if not practical, you may opt to use duff, boughs, or other similar material as insulation for your bed.

4

Shelter

Our communities are filled with homes made of brick and lumber—what would life be like without the turnkey home?

> *The first four days we went without sleep trying to meet the demands Mark placed upon us. We created a camp with improvised benches, shelters, drying racks, and a community center. Although a far cry from my home in Cheney, it provided ample protection from the harsh winter weather.*

WHERE TO BUILD A SHELTER

Since you intend to stay, it is important that the resources needed to live are close. Abundant edible vegetation and a clean water source are essential. The ideal site will be on level ground and have a southern exposure if it's north of the equator and a northern exposure if south of it; this allows for optimal light and heat from the sun throughout the day. In addition, build your shelter so the entrance faces east, which allows for best early morning sun exposure.

When selecting your site, don't forget to avoid the various environmental hazards that can wipe out all your hard work in just a matter of seconds. These hazards are: avalanche slopes, drainage and dry riverbeds with a potential for flash floods (if near bodies of water, stay above tidemarks), rock formations that might collapse, dead trees that might blow down, overhanging dead limbs, and large-animal trails.

THE BASICS OF SHELTER DESIGN

The exact type of shelter you build is determined by a multitude of variables. These include your climate and environment, available man-made and natural materials, your imagination, and your abilities as a builder.

As with any improvised item, you should construct your shelter so that it is safe and durable. Poles need to be strong enough to support the overall shelter. In most cases, the shelter's skeletal makeup is created by lashing three or four poles together and then placing additional poles (boughs, bark, sod, and so on) on top. When the basic shelter is done, it needs to be solid enough to withstand the elements: wind, rain, heat, and cold. To help meet these criteria, use a 45- to 60-degree pitch on all roofs or leaning walls. In addition, the roof (or shelter covering) needs to have an appropriate depth. Inside the shelter there should be enough room for storage of dry wood, food, and gear. If you have a fire in or near the shelter, be sure to provide appropriate ventilation and to build it in an area that has been cleared of flammable materials.

When building your shelter, various lashings may be needed to hold the structure together. Two are listed below.

THE SHEAR LASH

This lash is best used when making a bipod or tripod structure. Lay the poles side by side, attach the line to one of the poles (a clove hitch will work), run the line around all the poles three times (called a wrap). Next, run the line two times between each of the parallel poles (called a frap). It should go around and over the wrap. Make sure to pull it snug each time. Finish by tying another clove hitch.

THE SQUARE LASH

The square lash is used to join poles at right angles. As with the shear lash, start with a clove hitch. Wrap the line, in a box pattern, over and under the poles—alternating between each pole. After you have done this three times,

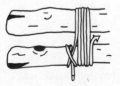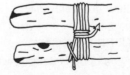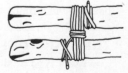

Shear lash.

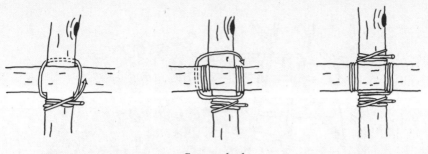

Square lash.

tightly run several fraps between the two poles and over the preceding wrap. Pull it snug and finish with a clove hitch.

PRIMITIVE SHELTERS

In an emergency, use any available natural shelter or quickly improvise a tarp shelter. A tree well, root buttress, or cave will serve you well for the night. For more long-term primitive shelters, consider the following options.

OPPOSING LEAN-TO

A large opposing lean-to can easily be built by using natural materials commonly found in warm temperate and snow environments. A double lean-to provides protection from all directions. This shelter is usually made for a single family but can be built large enough to house twenty to thirty people.

Find two trees approximately 12 to 18 feet apart with forked branches 8 to 10 feet high on each trunk. Break away any other branches that pose a safety threat or interfere with the construction process. In addition, be sure to clear any saplings, duff, or wood that is between the two trees and may interfere with the actual shelter site. Place a ridgepole (a strong pole that is long enough to span the distance between the two trees and 4 inches in diameter) into the forked branches. *Note:* If unable to find two trees with forked branches, use a square lash to attach the ridgepole to the trees.

Lay several support poles across the ridgepole (on each side) at a 45- to 60-degree angle to the ground. Support poles need to be 15 to 18 feet long and placed 1 to 2 feet apart. Be sure to incorporate the front and back into the framework, leaving enough room for a small doorway on one side. The

Opposing lean-to.

door will eventually be covered with a hide or other appropriate material. To create a stronger framework, weave small branches into the support poles (perpendicular).

Cover the entire shelter with 12 to 18 inches of bark, moss, boughs, and so forth. The material should be placed in a layered fashion, starting at the bottom. If you plan on having fires inside the shelter, be sure to leave a vent hole at the top. Consult the section on roofs for other options on how to roof primitive shelters.

WICKIUP

The wickiup shelter is common in areas where building materials are scarce. This shelter can be used anywhere that poles, brush, leaves, grass, or boughs can be found. The wickiup is not the ideal shelter for areas where prolonged rains prevail but if the insulation material is heaped on thick, it will provide adequate protection from most elements. A large wickiup can easily house up to eight people.

Gather three strong 15- to 20-foot poles (to create a 14-foot floor space and enough room to accommodate eight people) and use a shear lash to connect them together at the top. *Note:* If one or more of the three poles has a fork at its top, it may not be necessary to lash them together. Spread the poles out until a tripod is formed and they can stand without support. A 60-degree angle is optimal. Using additional poles, fill in all the sides by leaning them against the top of the tripod. Don't discard shorter poles; they can be used in the final stages of this process. Make sure you leave a small entrance that can later be covered with a hide or other appropriate material.

For immediate action, cover the shelter with brush, leaves, reeds, bark, and so forth. For additional protection, layer the roofing materials in the following design: Starting at the bottom, cover the framework with boughs, grass, and/or plant stalks. Next, cover it from the bottom to top with mulch and/or dirt. Finally, to hold the roof material in place, lay poles on top and around the wickiup. Be sure to leave a vent hole at the top, if you plan on having fires inside the shelter.

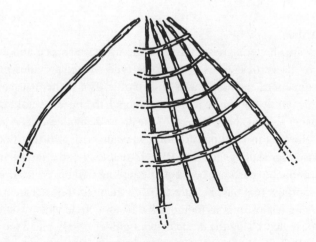

Wickiup framework.

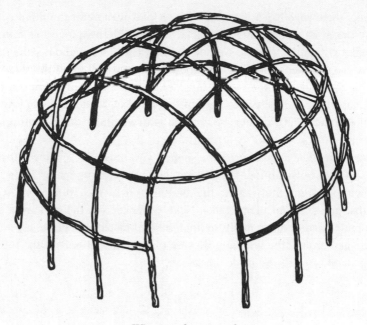

Wigwam framework.

WIGWAM

The wigwam shelter's greatest asset is the increased space and headroom created by its vertical walls. This dome-type shelter provides protection from all directions and has a lower wind profile. The shelter is usually made for a single family but can be built large enough to house several families by simply using an oval shape instead of the dome design described here.

The following instructions are for a wigwam with a 10-foot floor space. Cut twenty-four saplings that are 10 to 15 feet long and 2 inches in diameter. Willow and maple work best but any sapling will do. *Note:* If unable to use the saplings that day, be sure to store them so they are bent into a U shape. Using a stick or your foot, mark a 10-foot circle where you intend to place the shelter. Using the circle as your guide, evenly place the saplings around it. Bury the large end of each sapling 6 to 10 inches into the ground and tap dirt around it to help hold it in place. *Note:* To establish the hole for the saplings, pound a solid wooden stake into the ground and then remove it. Next, create the basic framework by bending opposing saplings together (overlapping by at least 2 feet) and using a shear lash to hold them together. Once completed, the twenty-four poles should create a domelike structure with at least a 7-foot-high center. Using additional saplings, wrap them horizontally around the framework. Be sure to leave a 3- to 4-foot-high doorway that can later be covered with a hide or other appropriate material. For optimal roofing support place the horizontal poles 12 to 18 inches apart.

LOG CABIN (WITHOUT NOTCHES)

A log cabin is a long-term shelter that is most often used in cold and temperate climates. The logs provide a safe, stable, and insulated structure that delivers excellent protection from the elements. These structures can be built with an A-frame or lean-to-style roof. If you are alone and/or resources are limited, however, I recommend a lean-to roof design. When selecting logs to use, make sure the weight is not unmanageable. If alone, a log with a diameter of 6 inches or less is advised. The length of each log depends on your shelter size and on which wall it is going to be used.

Since the logs are not notched you will need to provide a framework that will hold them in place. Gather fourteen strong 8- to 10-foot poles. At each of the four corners bury three of the poles (twelve total poles used) 8 to 12 inches into the ground and tap dirt around them to help hold them in place. Two feet to the left of the front right corner place two more poles. The 2-foot area will become your doorway. *Note:* All support poles are placed so they can hold the horizontal logs that create the shelter's wall.

Once all the support poles are in place, stack the logs between them. Use a moderate amount of straw-and-mud mortar to help hold them in place and seal up any openings.

A straw-and-mud mortar can be made by thoroughly mixing an equal amount of mud with a fibrous material like dry grass, straw, or ferns. Once dry, the mixture acts like extremely strong glue.

The back wall should be about 5 to 6 feet high and the front wall about 7 to 8 feet high. Run a log over the front wall and doorway so the sidewalls

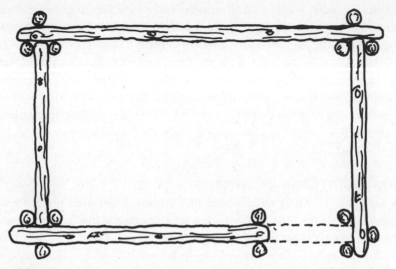

Building a log cabin that doesn't use notching requires the use of vertical poles to support the walls.

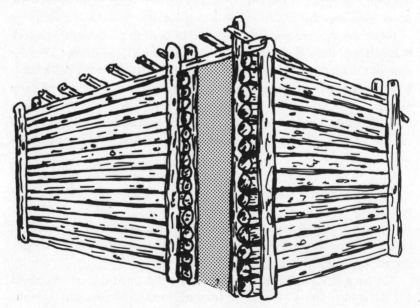

Log cabin shelter.

support it. Finish the walls by applying generous amounts of mortar inside and out.

Roof the shelter by placing logs side by side (perpendicular to the doorway) until it is covered. Fill in all openings with your mud mortar and cover it with boughs, sod, brush, or duff. If you intend to build a fire inside, make sure you provide an adequate ventilation hole that can be opened and closed. The door can be covered with any appropriate material or you may choose to build a wooden one out of your available resources.

SOD SHELTER
The sod shelter is most common in areas where there is a lack of trees. Sod is soil that has a strong root structure of grass or various vegetation holding it together. Sod can be used to build any number of shelter types—from a sod igloo to a small rectangular house. In most instances the sod is cut into 6- by 18-inch pieces of turf and laid in place like one might use a brick or block of packed snow. The roof will need a support structure stronger than the existing sod walls. Gather four poles that are approximately 10 feet long and vertically bury them 8–12 inches—one at each of the shelter's four corners. Tap dirt around them to make them more secure. Next, lash a pole to the top of the front two poles and another to the top of the back poles. Use the horizontal poles as the basic support structure for the roof. The roof may consist of poles laid side by side and lashed together, mats, thatching, or sod.

Sod shelter.

CAVE

A cave is the ultimate natural shelter. With very little effort it can provide protection from the various elements. Caves, however, are not without risk. Some of these risks include (but are not limited to) other animals, rodents, reptiles, and insects; bad air; slippery slopes, rocks, and crevasses; floods or high-water issues; combustible gases (most common where excessive bat droppings are noted). When using a cave as a shelter you should follow some basic rules:

• Never light a fire inside a small cave—it may use up oxygen and may cause an explosion if there are enough bat droppings present. Fires should be lit near the cave entrance where adequate ventilation is available.

• To avoid slipping into crevasses, getting lost, bad gas, and other hazards—never venture too far into the cave.

• Make sure the entrance is above the high-tide mark.

• Keep a constant awareness of water movement within a cave. If it appears to be prone to flooding—look for another shelter.

• Never enter or use old mines. The risk is not worth the benefit. Collapsing passages and vertical mine shafts are just a few of the potential problems.

• If possible, use a cave where the entrance faces the sun (south entrance if north of the equator; north entrance if south of the equator).

A wall can be built at the cave entrance by leaning support poles against it and covering them with grass or mat shingles. Be sure to leave an area large enough not only to build a fire, but also to provide adequate ventilation within the shelter.

TROPICAL HUT

These huts are common in tropical regions, swamps, or areas that have excessive amounts of rain. The elevated bed/floor provides protection from the moist or water-covered ground while the overhead roof keeps you dry.

To construct a small tropical hut, pound four poles (8 to 12 feet long) 8 to 12 inches into the ground at each of the shelter's four corners. Tap dirt around it to make it more secure. Create the floor by lashing a strong pole 2 feet off the ground on each side of the shelter so that it connects the rectanglular or square base together. Next, create a solid platform by laying additional poles on top of and perpendicular to the side poles. Make sure

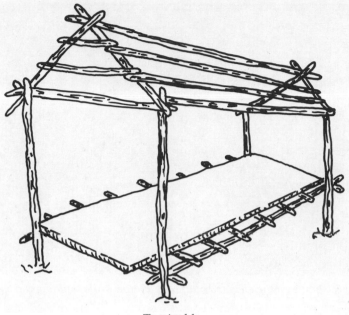

Tropical hut.

that all the poles are strong enough to support your weight. Finish the floor by using a mat (discussed later) or moss, grass, leaves, and/or branches. *Note:* For a large shelter these principles are still used but you'll need additional vertical poles to support the structure.

The roof is created using the same support poles used to build the floor. An A-frame cover works best. Make two triangles by lashing three poles together (six poles creating two triangles). The base of each triangle needs to be long enough to span the distance between the two main support poles (front and back). Next lash the base of the triangle to the top of the hut's vertical support poles. Find a sturdy pole that will span the length of your roof and place it on top of the two triangles. Lash in place. Additional roof support beams should be lashed down the sides of the triangle until an appropriate roof framework has been created. Cover (shingle) the roof with large overlapping leaves or other appropriate shingling material.

Bill Frye stands on the elevated platform created while building a tropical hut.

SNOW CAVE

Snow caves are most often used in the warm temperate (winter) and snow environments. Although a snow cave provides good protection from the elements, it is small and not appropriate for large groups. When constructing the cave, take care not to overheat or get wet.

Find an area with firm snow to a depth of at least 6 feet. A steep slope such as a snowdrift will suffice, provided there is no risk of an avalanche). Dig an entryway into the slope deep enough to start a tunnel (approximately 3 feet) and wide enough for you to fit into. Since cold air sinks, construct a snow platform 2 to 3 feet above the entryway. It should be flat, level, and large enough for you to comfortably lie down on. Using the entryway as a starting point, hollow out a domed area that is large enough for you and your equipment. To prevent the ceiling from settling or falling in, create a high domed roof. To prevent asphyxiation, make a ventilation hole in the roof. If available, insert a stick or pole through the hole so that it can be cleared periodically. To further protect the shelter from the elements, place a block of snow in the entryway. Check the entrance periodically.

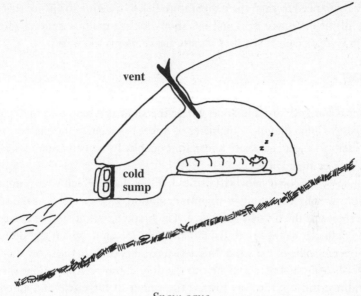

Snow cave.

During a winter class, Greg Cattin and Dr. Kennan Buechter built and slept in a snow cave.

You will need to keep the temperature below freezing to ensure that the walls of the cave stay firm and the snow doesn't melt. A general rule of thumb is if you cannot see your breath, the shelter is too warm.

IGLOO

An igloo can provide a long-term winter shelter for a small family. This shelter is normally used in areas where the snow is windblown and firmly packed. An igloo that has a diameter of 8 feet is adequate for one person; a diameter of 12 feet can easily house four people. Its construction requires a snow saw or large knife.

Find a windblown snowdrift or field, 2 feet deep, which when support-ing your weight leaves only a slight indentation. Draw a circle in the snow that represents the desired igloo size. The marked outline will become the inside diameter of the igloo. Establish a door location, which should be at a 90-degree angle to the wind. Make two parallel lines in the snow that are 30 inches apart and perpendicular to the door entrance. These lines should extend one-third of the way toward the center of the circle and an equal distance away. This area will eventually become your entrance, cooking, and storage area. It also will serve as a cold sump for the shelter. Using the

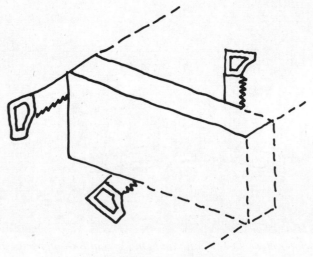

Cutting a snow block.

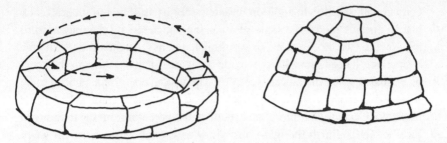

Constructing an igloo is a time-consuming process.

two lines as your guide, cut blocks that measure 30 inches long, 15 inches deep, and 8–12 inches thick. Start at the outside of the circle and continue until the two parallel lines end (one-third of the way to the center of the circle). Set the blocks aside. In order to finish the shelter you will need to acquire additional blocks from another location. Once all the blocks are cut you can begin building the igloo.

Start by placing four full-sized blocks, side by side, on the outside of the circle. Next, make a diagonal cut that runs from the ground of the second block to the top of the fourth. The fifth and following blocks will be the standard 15-inch height. The slope will provide a spiral effect that makes the construction easier and provides stability to the igloo. Continue adding blocks until the first layer is complete. As your dome begins to take form, trim the blocks (see diagram) and tilt them slightly inward to increase the

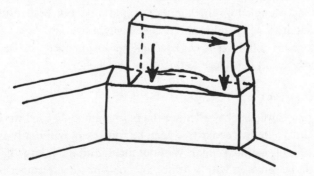

As the dome begins to take shape, trim the blocks.

contact and stability. In addition, greater stability is obtained if each block placed doesn't end on the same seam as the one below it (you may need to trim one or two blocks to make sure this happens). As the dome wall gets higher, you'll need to work from inside the igloo—leaving through the doorway created when the blocks were cut. The last layers of blocks need to be trimmed at an angle so the key block can be positioned on top. The key, or final, block is the centerpiece. It is round and tapered in from the top toward the shelter. To finish the igloo, use snow as the mortar to close all weak areas. In addition, if you want to increase the insulation of the shelter—simply pile more snow around it. If you intend to have a small fire (remember the rule about seeing your breath), don't forget a vent hole.

PRIMITIVE SHELTERS: ROOFS
Most primitive shelters require some sort of improvised roof placed over the framework in a shingling design. To shingle, place the material from bottom to top so the higher rows overlap those below by about one-third. The following roofing options can be used to cover most shelter designs.

BIRCH AND ELM BARK SHINGLES
Birch and elm bark are the most common types of bark used for covering a shelter. Large pieces of bark can easily be cut (use a knife and make a rectangular cut from top to bottom) and stripped from a tree or log. Be sure to peel the bark off along the vertical cut. If you experience difficulty removing the bark, beating the area with a log will help release it from the tree. Once the bark is removed, lay it flat on the ground with rocks, wood, and so on and allow it to dry. When dry, the bark can be lashed to the horizontal beams and shingled up the shelter's framework. For best results, the shingles that are side by side should have a slight overlap. *Note:* You can sew bark together if the size is not adequate for its intended use. Be sure to leave a smoke (vent) hole close to the top of the shelter.

WOOD SHINGLES
Straight-grained woods like cedar are the most commonly used wood roofing material. Where live cedar trees can be found you will easily find old fallen, dead, and seasoned cedar. Without much difficulty, large half-inch shingles can be removed with a knife, axe, or—in some instances—with

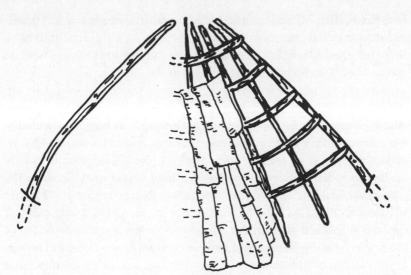

Bark shingles.

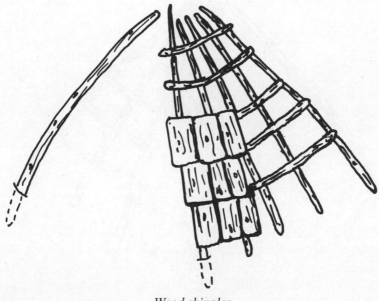

Wood shingles.

bare hands. The soft wood can be lashed or nailed to the horizontal beams and shingled up the shelter's framework. If lashed, you'll need to drill holes in the top of each shingle. Use an awl-like tool to perform this easy task. Be sure to leave a smoke hole close to the top of the shelter.

GRASS ROOFING
Although grass can be used as a roofing material, its biggest downfall is the amount of time required to harvest enough to cover a shelter. Ideally, collect tall, dry grass that grew the previous year. Older grass is usually brittle and rotted and new grass must be dried before used. Separate the grass into small bundles (with the root ends together) that are 1 to 2 inches in diameter. Place the bundles close to one another. Fold a long piece of cordage in half and place it approximately 4 inches down from the top of the first bundle. Tie an overhand knot, slide in another bundle, and repeat. If you run out of line before you reach the end, simply tie another piece

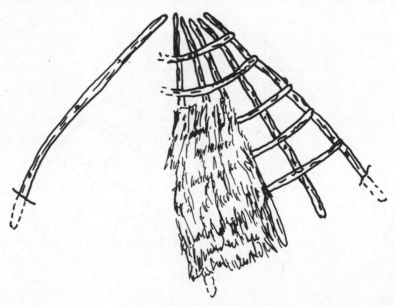

Grass roofing.

Mat roofing.

to the first and continue the process. At the same time, tie a second line approximately 3 to 4 inches below the first. Once you have enough of the grass skirts to cover the shelter, lash them to the framework. Be sure to use proper shingling techniques as you go up the shelter. Don't forget to leave a smoke hole close to the top of the shelter.

MAT ROOFING

A mat made by weaving together cattail stalks or leaves, reeds, or yucca leaves provides a strong covering for most shelters. Similar to the grass matting, these mats are made and then attached to the shelter. Begin by laying your material down on the ground. To create a tighter fit, alternate the stalks' thick and skinny ends. Fold a long piece of cordage in half and place it approximately 4 inches down from the top of the first stalk. Tie an overhand knot, slide in another stalk, and repeat. If you run out of line before you reach the end of the mat, simply tie another piece to the first and continue the process. Once the first row is done, perform the same process approximately every 4 inches (down the mat) until you reach the bottom.

THE FIRE PIT

Since the shelter you build will become your home, creating an area for fire is important. The fire provides light, heat, cooking, and entertainment. If not used wisely, fire can cause burns and may even kill you. Before lighting any fire in your shelter, ensure there is enough ventilation to allow the smoke to escape and help prevent asphyxiation. A good fire pit is normally placed between the door and the center of the shelter. This location allows the back of the shelter to be used. For best results, dig a 2- to 3-foot circular fire pit that is approximately 8 inches deep and line the bottom and sides with stones. *Caution:* Be sure not to use stones from riverbeds or those that appear to retain moisture. The stones will hold the fire's heat, help prevent sparks from flying across the shelter and onto your sleeping mat, and ensure adequate oxygen circulates under the fire. To decrease the smoke within your house, use wood that is less apt to smoke—dry, without bark or lichen, and pitch free.

INCREASING INSULATION

Creating a second wall—inside or out—around the shelter will increase its ability to keep you warm (or cool). Use the same double wall principle on your ceiling and decrease the amount of moisture that leaks into the shelter.

Doing something as easy as tying mats, hides, or grass skirts to the interior walls can create the second wall. To make an elaborate insulation wall: drive a row of tall stakes (about 1 foot apart) 6 to 8 inches into the ground and 12 to 18 inches from the shelter wall; next, weave willow branches or other similar material between and perpendicular to the stakes; and finish by filling the structure with grass, duff, or leaves. To increase the roof's insulation, use a mat or hide and run it below the roof. Hold it in place by attaching it to the sidewalls.

SHELTER DRAINAGE

The ideal solution to drainage problems is to build your shelter so that it sits slightly higher than the surrounding ground. If this is not possible, however, it takes only a few minutes to dig a trench around your shelter and the benefit will make it a worthwhile process. The small trench should fall directly below the roof's ends and follow the ground's natural pitch until the water is directed far away from your home. This design works

Insulated walls help create a shelter that is cooler in the summer and warmer in the winter.

similar to the gutters seen on a modern home. The trench collects the water and via a small slope that extends from one end to another it directs the water away from the house.

FURNITURE

Furniture may or may not be a concern. Mats (as described in the preceding section on roofs) can be used as bedding or for sitting on. Beds, tables, and other elevated furniture can be constructed using the same principles described in the tropical hut section. Don't limit yourself—poles and cordage are the only tools you'll need to build a variety of furniture items.

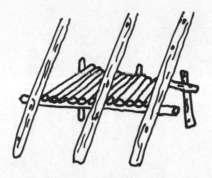

A bed or table help make your shelter a home.

BEDS AND TABLES

To construct a small table or bed, pound two poles (3 to 5 feet long) 8 to 12 inches into the ground as close to the shelter's wall as needed to create the end result (appropriate width for your table or bed). The shelter's wall should provide the support for the other side of your design but if you don't think it can, place two additional poles close to the wall. To establish the hole for the poles, pound a solid wooden stake into the ground and then remove it. Secure the poles into the ground by tapping dirt around them. Lash strong poles (2 feet off the ground for a bed or 3 to 4 feet for a table) on each of the four sides of the upright poles. Next, create a solid platform by laying additional poles on top of and perpendicular to the side poles. If a bed, make sure that all the poles are strong enough to support your weight. Also, if a bed, cover it with a mat, moss, grass, leaves, or perhaps branches. For added support, lash a diagonal pole at each of the far ends of the structure.

CHAIRS

If you know how to make a tripod, you can easily convert it into a chair. To make a tripod, lay three 7- to 8-foot poles side by side and lash them together. Stand them up and place the legs out until you can assume a sitting position without hitting your head or feeling cramped between the poles. Lash poles to the legs at a height that allows you to sit with your feet touching the ground. Next, create a solid platform by laying additional poles on top of and basically perpendicular to the side poles. Realize that

Bill Frye sits on a quickly improvised bench.

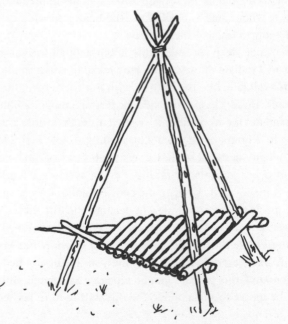

It is easy to turn a tripod into a chair.

Fire bed.

one of the three side poles will be considered the front of the chair and it should be parallel to these platform poles. If a backing is desired, it can be created by tying a large thick piece of buckskin toward the top of the back leg and to the front two legs with a thong. To help reduce the risk of tearing my hide, I usually place a thick piece of rawhide on each side of the buckskin's hole and thread the thong through all three pieces. In addition, to prevent tearing, don't use the backing to support your whole weight.

FIRE BED

In extremely cold temperate or desert environments a fire bed will help keep you warm during the night. It takes about 2 hours to prepare. Used in large shelters or when none is available—the heat generated from these beds has been know to last as long as 2 days.

Dig a 4- to 6-inch-deep rectangle that is big enough for you to lie in. Since the heat will radiate outward, you may make the area smaller if digging is hard. If available, line the bottom with flat rocks (avoid rocks that contain moisture). Build a long fire inside the large rectangular hole. As the fire grows, spread out the wood until it evenly covers the whole area and let it burn for 1½ to 2 hours before you stop feeding it new fuel. Once only coals remain, spread them out so they cover the bottom of the hole evenly. Next, place dirt over the coals, stamping it down as you go, until there is approximately 4 inches of it covering the bed. To make sure the dirt covering is enough, push your whole index finger into the dirt that is over the coals. If you get burned, add more dirt. Finally, cover the fire bed with an insulating material like duff, boughs, leaves, and so on. *Note:* Make sure there aren't any loose embers that may ignite your insulation bed. Once a bed has been created, this process can be repeated as needed. Subsequent fire beds will be easier to make since the dirt will require less energy to remove.

5

Fire

Our homes are heated with gas or electric furnaces—what would life be like without an adjustable thermostat?

> *It only took me five seconds to appreciate how cold 80 degrees below zero really was. How could I be expected to meet my needs under these conditions? An immediate action shelter and fire had never been so important! I moved quickly and within minutes had a large chest-high fire made from dead branches (found on the bottom of standing trees) and heartwood. The fire not only kept me warm while I built my shelter, it also motivated me throughout the process. As night fell I asked myself "What if I hadn't had my metal match to start the fire?" The impact of that day left me yearning to learn more about the art of primitive fire-building.*

PURPOSE OF FIRE

The use of fire is unlimited and a must for long-term survival and wilderness living. It provides light, warmth, and comfort; a source of heat for cooking, purifying water, and drying clothing; and smoke for de-scenting snares and tanning hides.

SITE SELECTION AND PREPARATION

Your fire circle should be on flat and level ground, close to your shelter (not too close) and fire materials, and in a location that provides adequate protection from the elements. The site should be prepared by clearing a 10-foot fire circle (scrape away all leaves and brush) to prevent the fire from spreading into the forest. If you intend to have your fire inside your shelter, be sure the shelter is vented and a fire pit has been created (covered in chapter 4).

A REVIEW OF BASIC FIRE PRINCIPLES

All three sides of the fire triangle must be present for a fire to work. Recall that these are heat, oxygen, and fuel. Fuel is broken down into tinder, kindling, and fuel; oxygen is created through the use of a platform and brace; and heat is obtained from a spark that will ignite your tinder. Much of this has been discussed in chapter 1 and in my book, *Wilderness Survival*. At this time, however, I'd like to expand upon fuel procurement and preparation along with several methods of primitive heat sources.

FUEL

Fuel is any material, thumb-size or bigger, that will burn slowly and steadily once lit. A number of fuel sources might be available in the wild:

• Dry, dead branches found at the bottom of trees: this material is great during dry or very cold weather. It provides all of the various stages of fuel when it's broken down properly. The biggest problems found with this fuel are during wet or extremely cold conditions. If the branches are wet, you'll need to prepare them by scraping off all of the wet bark and lichen. Running your knife across the wood's surface, at a 90-degree angle, can do this. If it is still too wet, split the wood to expose its inner dry material. If the weather is really cold the branches may break off even if green. Trying to burn a green branch may present a problem. To ensure it is dead, look for the absence of a meaty cambium layer that is found between the bark and the inner wood. If it is present, the branch is green and should not be used.

• Heartwood: heartwood requires a lot more energy and time when used to build a fire. It is ideal, however, during wet conditions when you need a dry surface that will easily ignite. The best source can be found in a stump that has a sharp-pointed top, in other words, a stump that wasn't created with a chainsaw. Stumps that have a flat surface absorb massive amounts of moisture (especially when capped with snow). To gather heartwood, pull, kick, or rip the pieces off the stump. If unable to separate the wood from the stump, use a pry pole (a sturdy pole that is wedged between the stump and its loose piece of wood) or your large fixed-blade knife to help it along. Once gathered, break the wood down from large to small.

• Animal dung: herbivores produce a great source of fuel in their dung, which is often used by individuals who live in the deserts and Great Plains.

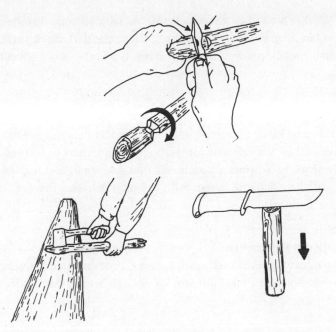

Methods of safely exposing the inner dry wood of a wet branch.

Since these animals eat grassy substances, they provide an excellent fuel log when their dung is dry. Breaking the dung into various sizes (tinder, kindling, and fuel) will ensure your success. I consider them Mother Nature's Presto Logs.

• Dry grasses: dry grass is not only great tinder but also provides an excellent fuel when tied into bundles. If this is my only source of fuel, I tie the grass into bundles that are 12 to 24 inches long with varying diameters. This allows me to stage my fire up from small to big.

• Green wood: if you have a hot fire, green wood that is finely split will burn. This should not be used, however, in the early stages of your fire. To increase your odds of success, remove the outer bark and moist cambium layer.

• Seal blubber: a square foot of seal blubber will burn for several hours. To use, place the fur side down and ignite the raw side using either a heat tablet or other hot and long-lasting tinder. As with all animal products, it is best to burn them in a well-vented area. Since the dark black smoke from seal blubber tends to stain skin and clothing, it is best to avoid direct contact with it.

HEAT
In a wilderness living environment, matches and lighters will eventually fail or run out. Thus other options for starting your fire must be learned. These include spark-based (metal match and flint and steel) and friction-based (hand drill, bow and drill, pump drill, fire plow, bamboo fire saw, and fire thong) heat sources.

Spark-Based Heat Source
The two most commonly used spark systems for starting a fire are the metal match (sparker) and flint. Both provide enough heat to start tinder from a spark.

A student strikes her tinder with a metal match.

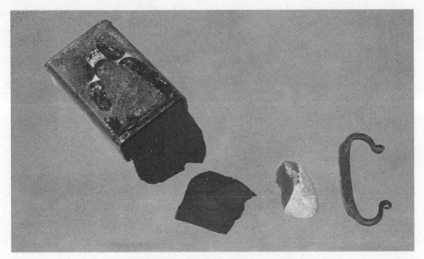

Flint and steel and charred cloth

Metal Match

A metal match (sparker) is a man-made flint similar to the one found in a cigarette lighter. It is shaped like a cylinder with a diameter of approximately ¼ inch and a length from 2 to 4 inches. To use a metal match, place it firmly in the center of the properly prepared tinder and with a firm controlled downward stroke, run a blade (knife or similar object) at a 45- to 90-degree angle down the sparker. The resultant spark should provide enough heat to ignite the tinder; however, it may take several attempts. If after five tries it has not lit, the tinder should be reworked in the palm of your hand or with a knife to ensure that adequate edges are exposed and oxygen is able to flow within it.

Flint and Steel

This is an effective method for starting fires, but the necessary materials may be hard to find. Some flint options are quartzite, iron pyrite, agate, or jasper. Any steel can be used with the flint, but most people use an old file. By striking the iron particles, heat is created when they are crushed and torn away. The best tinder to use is charred cloth, which can be created by placing several 2-inch squares of cotton cloth inside a tin can with ventilation holes in its top that is then put in a fire's coals for 15 to 30 minutes. It is done when smoke stops coming out of the holes. Be sure to turn the can every couple minutes.

To use the flint and steel, hold the flint in one hand and as close to the tinder as possible. With the steel in your other hand, strike downward onto the flint. Direct the resulting spark into the center of the charred cloth. Consult the section on tinder for information on how to light tinder with the coal created using a friction-based technique.

Friction-Based Heat Sources

Friction-based heat works through a process of pulverizing and heating appropriate woods, until a fine char is created. The char can be used to ignite awaiting tinder. A circular technique (hand drill, bow and drill, or pump drill) or the less often used friction methods (fire plow, bamboo fire saw, or fire thong) can be used to create char. The biggest problems associated with these techniques are muscle fatigue, poor wood selection, and moisture that prevents the material from reaching an appropriate temperature.

Bow and Drill

The bow and drill is often used when the spindle and baseboard materials are not good enough to create a char when using a hand drill technique. The bow helps establish the friction that is needed in order to use materials that would otherwise be inferior. In addition, it is useful when bad weather is adversely affecting your ability to create a char with an appropriate hand drill. A bow and drill is composed of four separate parts:

• Bow: a 3- to 4-foot branch of hardwood that is seasoned, stout, slightly curved, about ¾ inch in diameter, and with a small fork at one end. A strong line, attached to the bow, is necessary to create enough tension to turn the spindle once it is inserted. Leather, parachute line, shoelace, or improvised cordage can be used. Securely attach the line to one end of the bow. Ideally, drill a hole through the bow, tie a knot on the line, and then run the line through the hole. The knot ensures that the line will not slip or slide forward and since the line's tension will inevitably loosen it allows you to make quick adjustments. Use a fixed loop to attach the line's free end to the fork on the other side. If the bow doesn't have a fork, create one by carving a notch at the appropriate place.

• Cup: made from hardwoods, antlers, rocks, or pitch wood, the cup has a socket for the top of the spindle. The cup's purpose is to hold the spindle in place while it is turned by the bow. In order to decrease the friction between the cup and the spindle, when using a deadwood you must lubricate the cup's socket. You can use body oils or animal fat to accomplish this.

• Spindle: a smooth straight cylinder made from a dry softwood that is approximately ¾ inch in diameter and 8 to 12 inches long. The ideal spindle is made from yucca, sotol (a variation of yucca), cottonwood, aspen, willow, sage, or cacti. The smaller dead branches of cedar, locust, and ash are also appropriate for use as spindles. The best way to evaluate the material is to press on it with a fingernail—if it indents, it should work. To prepare the spindle for use, carve both ends so that one is cone shaped and smooth and the other is round with rough edges.

• Fire board: should be made from a material similar, but not identical, in hardness to the spindle. The ideal fire board is 15 to 18 inches long, ¾ inch thick, and 2 to 3 inches wide.

Preparing the Fire Board for Use

• Carve a circular socket (three-quarters of the diameter of the spindle) at least 4 inches from one end, close to the long side (but not right on the side), and about one-quarter of the thickness of the board. If the socket is too close to the side, there will not be enough material to prevent the spindle from kicking out of the hole.

• Prime the hole: twist the bowline around the spindle so that the coned end is up and the rounded blunt end is down. If it doesn't feel like it wants to twist out, then the bow's line needs to be tightened. While holding the bow and spindle together, kneel on your right knee and place your left foot on the fire board. Insert the cone end of the spindle inside the cup, and place the round, blunt end into the fire board socket that you created with your knife. Holding the bow in the right hand (at the end) and the cup in the left, apply gentle downward pressure on the spindle. The spindle should be perpendicular to the ground. For added support and stability, rest the left arm and elbow around and upon the left knee and shin. (If left-handed, put the bow in your left hand, the cup in your right, and kneel on your left knee instead of the right.) With a straightened arm, begin moving the bow back and forth with a slow, even, steady stroke. Once the friction between the spindle and the fire board begins to create smoke, gradually increase the downward pressure and continue until a smooth round dent is made in the fire board.

• Using your knife or saw cut a pie-shaped notch through the entire thickness of the fire board so that its point stops slightly short of the hole's center.

Bow and Drill Technique

Once the separate parts of the bow and drill are prepared, it is then ready. To use it, simply apply the same technique shown for preparing the fire board (priming the hole). Once the smoke is billowing out and you can't go any longer, check for a coal. The coal should have been created from the friction and can be found within or below the fire board's notch. Be sure to place a piece of bark, leather, or other appropriate material under your baseboard for the coal to sit on. This will protect it from the moist ground and help you move it to your tinder. Once you have an ember, remember to relax and take

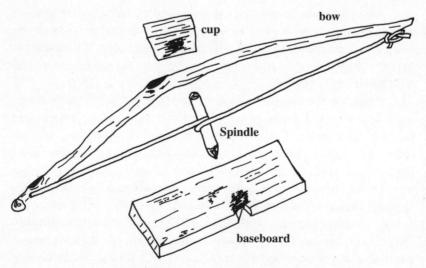

The various parts of a bow and drill.

The author uses a cedar spindle and baseboard to create a coal from a bow and drill.

your time. Don't blow on the coal. The moisture from your mouth may put it out. If you feel it needs more oxygen just gently fan it with your hand. In most cases, however, simply waiting a few seconds will allow the ember to begin to glow.

Hand Drill

The hand drill is similar to the bow and drill except you use your hands to turn the spindle. This method is used when conditions are ideal—no moisture in the air and you have the best materials at your disposal. The hand drill is composed of two parts:

 • Spindle: a smooth straight cylinder made from a dry softwood that is approximately ½ to ¾ inch in diameter and 2 to 3 feet long. The ideal spindle is made from yucca or sotol (a variation of yucca). I have heard reports of people using cattail or mullein but these materials are finicky at best. To prepare the spindle for use, carve the fatter end so that it is round with rough edges. *Note:* Keeping the fat end down helps increase the fric-

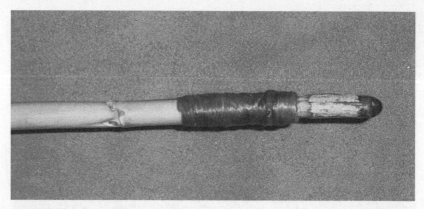

To make this hand drill, insert a sotol plug into a bamboo shaft, allowing optimal use of the sotol.

tion between your spindle and fire board (as your hand moves down the spindle).

At times it may be hard to find a straight spindle. In situations like this, I use a piece of bamboo as the shaft and create a plug from the short piece of sotol (or other material) that fits inside the end. To help protect the end from splitting, I wrap it with sinew. If you do this, leave 2 to 3 inches of the plug extending beyond the end of the straight shaft. You could also use this technique to drill holes by replacing the friction plug with a stone bit.

• Fire board: the fire board is created from a softwood of similar (but not identical) hardness to the spindle. My favorites are yucca and sagebrush. The optimal size is 15 to 18 inches long, 2 to 3 inches wide, and ½ to ¾ inch thick. A notch will have to be prepared in a fashion similar to that described for the bow and drill.

The positioning techniques used for a hand drill vary from one person to another. Some sit while others kneel. Either way, the key is to be comfortable while still able to turn the spindle and apply appropriate downward pressure.

Hand Drill Technique
While sitting or kneeling, rub the spindle between your hands. In order to optimize the number of revolutions the spindle has, be sure you start at the

top and use as much of the hand (from heel to fingertip) as you can. Apply downward pressure, as your hands move down the spindle, until you reach bottom and then quickly move both hands up while ensuring that the spindle and fire board maintain contact at all times. Since the spindle will cool rapidly, this step is very crucial to your success. When the set begins to smoke, increase your speed and downward pressure until you can't go anymore. Just before I finish, I like to push the top of the spindle slightly away from the fire board's notch to help push out the coal. It's the revolutions in conjunction with the downward pressure that produces the friction needed to create a coal. Be sure to place a piece of bark, leather, or other appropriate material under your baseboard for the coal to sit on. This will protect it from the moist ground and help you move it to your tinder. Once you have an ember, remember to relax and take your time. Don't blow on the coal. The moisture from your mouth may put it out. If you feel it needs more oxygen, gently fan it with your hand. In most cases, however, simply waiting a few seconds will allow the ember to begin to glow.

Creating a coal using a sotol hand drill

At times it may be necessary to create additional downward pressure on your spindle. Two methods that are commonly used are:

* A mouthpiece: similar to the cup of a bow and drill but instead of using your hands to hold it on the spindle you use your teeth. When using this technique, shorten the spindle to 18 to 24 inches in length.

* A thumb thong: tie a thumb loop at each end of a thong and attach its center to the top of the spindle. By sliding your thumbs into the loops you are able to provide a nonstop spin with increased downward pressure. As with the mouthpiece, this technique will require you to use a shorter spindle.

Pump Drill

In addition to drilling holes, a pump drill can also be adapted into a friction heat source that works similar to the bow and drill. It consists of a spindle, crosspiece, flywheel, and fire board.

* Spindle: a piece of straight debarked hardwood that measures approximately 30 inches long with a diameter of 1⅛ inches on one end tapering to about ⅞ inch on the other. On the wider end, drill a 1- to 2-inch-deep hole (slightly bigger then ½ inch in diameter) into its exact center. This can be started with a hand drill that utilizes a ½-inch stone bit (discussed earlier in this chapter) and then finished by replacing the bit with a ½-inch wood plug of medium hardness. This technique should create a nicely rounded burned hole that has an equal diameter throughout its depth. (If the hole ends up not being centered, cut it off and start over.) Create a tip (plug) out of any of the spindle material previously mentioned. The ideal plug is made from yucca, sotol, cottonwood, aspen, willow, sage, cacti, cedar, locust, or ash. This plug should fit snuggly into the spindle's tip and extend 2 to 3 inches past the insertion point. Wrap sinew around the end of the spindle up about 3 inches of its shaft. This wrap not only secures the plug in place but it also helps prevent the end of the spindle from splitting. On the other end of the spindle, cut a ¼-inch notch into the center of the shaft. The string from the pump drill's crosspiece will ride there. To help protect the area, wrap the end with sinew from the bottom of the notch to about 1 inch down.

* Crosspiece: the crosspiece is a 1½- to 2-inch-wide piece of straight-grained hardwood (without knots) that measures between 22 and 24 inches in length. Create a hole in the exact center of the crosspiece that is ⅛ inch bigger around then the spindle. This can be done with your hand drill or

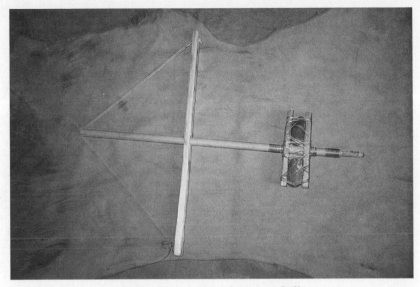

The various parts of a pump drill.

perhaps by using a hot coal. Tie a line to the far ends of the crosspiece so
that the line measures approximately 31 to 35 inches when measured from
one end to the other. When done, the crosspiece should easily slide up and
down the spindle and the line should fit within the spindle's notch.

• Flywheel: the flywheel sits on the lower end of the spindle providing balance and weight. The ideal flywheel weight for creating an ember
will be between 2½ and 3 pounds. To create it, gather two pieces of hardwood that are about 8 inches long by 2 inches wide and burn or drill a hole
into the exact center of each piece of wood. The size of the hole will depend
on the spindle's diameter. A proper fit allows the lower piece to wedge 4
inches up from the bottom of the spindle and the upper piece about 2½
inches above that. Next, find two rocks that weigh approximately 1¼ to 1½
pounds each and tie them between the two pieces of wood (one on each side
of the hole) making sure that the holes are exposed and are in line with
each other when done. Since it is doubtful the rocks will weigh exactly the
same, you may need to add twigs or line to one side of the flywheel to
balance it.

• Fire board: should be made from a material similar, but not identical, in hardness to the spindle plug. The ideal fire board is 15 to 18 inches long, ¾ inch thick, and 2 to 3 inches wide.

Pump Drill Technique

Place the plug inside the spindle and the flywheel, into position, over the top. Advance the crosspiece down the spindle letting the center of its line come to rest inside the upper notch. Prepare the fire board by carving a circular socket (three-quarters of the diameter of the spindle) at least 4 inches from one end, close to the long side (but not right on the side), and about one-quarter the thickness of the board. Place the spindle into the socket and turn it by hand until the line is wrapped around it and the crosspiece has moved up the shaft. At this point you are ready to begin.

Realize that this system is not much different from the bow and drill or hand drill. The spindle turns one way and then another while inside the fire board's socket. The constant rotation creates friction, which in turn creates heat and eventually a coal. As with both of the other systems, your technique will play a major role in success or failure.

Place one hand on each end of the crosspiece, kneel on your right knee, and place your left foot on the fire board. Apply a smooth yet forceful downward stroke that has a rapid acceleration early on. As the crosspiece gets close to the bottom, don't relax. Continue to apply downward pressure while the line is rewrapping itself around the spindle (in the opposite direction). By doing this you will maintain a friction force (contact) between the spindle and the fire board. Try to time it so that as the crosspiece reaches the top you can quickly accelerate back downward. Stop when a smooth round dent is made in the fire board and cut your notch in the same manner as explained under the bow and drill section. Once the notch is prepared, put bark, leather, or other dry material under your fire board to catch the coal. Place the spindle back in the notch and repeat the steps as just outlined until you have a solid wall of smoke and an ember is present. Once you have an ember, remember to relax and take your time. Don't blow on the coal. The moisture from your mouth may put it out. If you feel it needs more oxygen, gently fan it with your hand. In most cases, however, simply waiting a few seconds will allow the ember to begin to glow.

Fine-Tuning the Pump Drill
• Revolutions: the ideal number of revolutions per complete cycle (top to bottom to top) is around four (two down and two up). If you have too many more than that, the spindle loses its momentum, when going up, and, in turn, friction heat. Adjusting your string length will correct this problem.

The author uses a pump drill to start a fire. By simply changing to a rock bit, however, one could use it as a drill as well.

• Flywheel weight: although 2½ to 3 pounds is considered the ideal weight, this is not always true. To determine the best weight use the following guidelines. If your spindle plug produces a dark brown dust and ember, then it is just right. If it produces a light brown dust or no dust at all, then it is too light. If the spindle is destroyed during use or it goes through the fire board, then it is too heavy.

• Torque: in order to obtain a fluid motion during operation, the torque applied during the downward motion of the crosspiece needs to approximate the torque created during its upswing. Adjusting the string's position equally on both sides on the crosspiece will correct this problem. If you make an adjustment here, however, you may need to readjust the string's length to get your revolutions back to the desired setting.

Fire Plow

The fire plow is a method of literally rubbing two sticks together until a coal is created. This method is very difficult to master and takes a lot of practice. The best part about the fire plow is that no tools are required for its use and no notches need be created. Cottonwood or sotol are probably the two most often used woods in this technique. To make a fire plow you will need two pieces of wood:

• The plow (the piece you'll hold in your hand) should be about 1 foot long with one end approximately ¼ to ½ inch wide.

• The fire board needs to be around 2 inches wide and long enough for you to hold in place while moving the plow across it.

Fire Plow Technique

Place the plow at a 90-degree angle to the base and slowly begin pushing it back and forth creating a groove that is approximately 6 to 8 inches long. Place one hand close to the tip and the other at the butt end of the plow. Once you have a good groove established, lower the upper end of the plow—decreasing its angle and creating an increased area of contact between the plow and baseboard. Once the set is smoking well, slightly raise back up the butt end of the plow. By doing this you will intensify the heat on the tip. As you move the plow back and forth, be sure to make contact with the dust at least every other stroke. At first this may be difficult to

Fire plow.

do and you may find yourself pushing the dust out of the groove completely. Practice—sooner or later you'll find yourself with a coal at the end of your groove.

Bamboo Fire Saw

The fire saw is a technique most often used with hollow materials such as bamboo. It is composed of two pieces:

- Saw: cut a straight piece of the hollow material and sharpen the edge on one of its long sides.
- Baseboard: cut the hollow material in half (long ways) and then cut a notch across the width of its convex side. It is usually 12 inches in length.

Fire Saw Technique

The baseboard is the moving piece of the fire saw. Place well-prepared tinder in the concave side of the baseboard (in line with the notch you created) and hold it in place with a small twig or piece of the bamboo. Next, place the groove of the baseboard so that a cross is created between it and

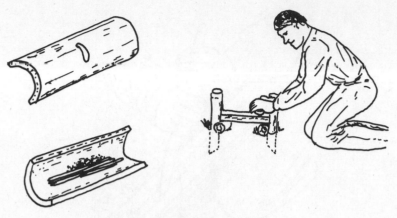

Bamboo fire saw.

the sharp end of the saw (which needs to be stationary). Begin moving the baseboard back and forth on the saw, increasing your speed as it begins to smoke and continue until you can't go any longer. The coal will form on the concave side of the baseboard within the awaiting tinder.

Fire Thong

The fire thong is a friction system that is often used in the tropics where rattan is abundant. It consists of two parts:

• Thong: made of twisted rattan that is 4 to 6 feet long and less than 1 inch in diameter.

• Baseboard: usually a deciduous material that is softer than the rattan and measures about 4 feet in length.

Fire Thong Technique

To use this method, a cross beam is needed to keep the baseboard off the ground and allow the thong to move freely across it. (See the following illustration.) It's the friction between the thong and the baseboard that creates the heat needed to produce a coal from this method. Be sure to place a piece of bark, leather, or other appropriate material under your baseboard for the coal to sit on. This will protect it from the moist ground and help you move it to your tinder.

Fire thong.

LIGHTING YOUR TINDER

When using a flint and steel, a bow and drill, a hand drill, a pump drill, a fire plow, a fire saw, or a fire thong, the resultant coal/ember can be used to ignite tinder. For success, use dry grass, lichen, or bark, such as juniper or cedar. To prepare the tinder, work it between your hands and fingers until it is a fine fluffy dry material that has edges and allows oxygen to circulate within it. Once done, mold it into a bird's nest and place any loose dust created from the process in the center of the nest. If you don't intend to use it right away, place it in your pocket or a dry plastic bag to prevent it from collecting moisture from the air.

Lighting a tinder using a coal from a friction-based heat source.

Once you have created a coal from any of the methods above—be patient. Don't rush—you have time. Don't blow on the coal. The moisture from your mouth may put it out. If you feel it needs more oxygen, gently fan it with your hand. In most cases, however, simply waiting a few seconds will allow the ember to begin its ever-so-pleasant glow. Once ready, gently move the coal into the center of the bird's nest and loosely fold the outer nest around it. Holding it all above your head, lightly blow on the coal—increasing in intensity—until the tinder ignites. To avoid burning your fingers, it may be necessary to hold the tinder between two sticks. Once the tinder ignites, place it on your platform next to the brace and begin building your fire.

FIRE REFLECTOR

Consider building a fire wall to reflect the fire's heat in the direction you want. Secure two poles into the ground 1 foot behind the fire circle. (Each pole should be approximately 3 feet high.) In order to pound the poles into the ground, you'll need to sharpen the ends and use a rock or another sturdy pole to drive them into the ground. Next, place two poles of similar size 4 to 6 inches in front of the others. Gather enough green logs of wrist diameter so that when placed between the poles they form a 3-foot-high wall. Depending on where you want the heat reflected, slightly lean the wall down or up to create the desired outcome.

HOLDING A COAL/FIRE

There are several methods commonly used to maintain a heat source for ongoing or later use.

KEEPING A FLAME

The best way to keep a flame is to provide an ongoing fuel source. The type of wood you use will directly affect this process. Softwoods provide an excellent light and heat source but they burn up rather fast. Softwoods con-

Fire reflector.

sist of woods like cedar, pine, and fir. Hardwoods like maple, ash, oak, and hickory will burn longer and produce less smoke. These woods are ideal for use at night.

KEEPING A COAL

Banking the Fire
If you are staying in one place, bank the fire to preserve its embers for use at a later time. Once you have a good bed of coals, cover them with ashes and/or dry dirt. If done properly, the fire's embers will still be smoldering in the morning. To rekindle the fire, remove the dry dirt, lay tinder on the coals, and gently fan them until the tinder ignites.

Fire Bundle
If you plan on traveling, use a fire bundle to transport the coal. A fire bundle has been known to save a coal from 6 to 12 hours. To construct it, surround the live coal with dry punk or fibrous bark like cedar or juniper—which is then surrounded by damp grass, leaves, or humus and finally by a heavy bark such as birch. The key to success is to ensure there is enough oxygen to keep the ember burning but not enough to promote its ignition. If the bundle begins to burn through it may be necessary to stop and build another fire from which to create another coal for transport.

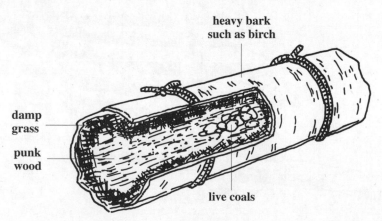

Fire bundle.

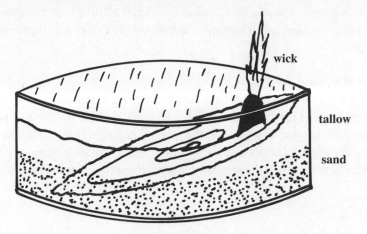

Fat lamp.

LAMPS AND STOVES

Fat Lamp

To create a fat lamp you will first need to render your animal fat into tallow. To do this, cook it over a low temperature until it is completely melted. It is common to have a few small particles left in the soup. To remove these particles, strain the liquid fat through a porous cloth. If you do not intend to use it immediately, store it in clean jars (fill close to the top), cover, and put in a cool dark place. The tallow can be used to meet many of your needs. It can be used as a lubricant, to make soap, or perhaps as a fuel for a fat lamp.

To create an oil lamp from tallow, use a small can that has its lid slightly attached at one end (a tuna can works great—clean it well). Bend the lid down so that it forms a 45-degree angle between the bottom of the can and where it is attached at the top. The lid will provide a platform for your wick. Fill the bottom third of the can with sand and fill it with liquid fat from that point to just below the top. Create a wick from any fluffy fibrous material. Some examples are milkweed seedpods, cattail seed heads, or perhaps even cotton. Fluff the wick up and set it on the lid platform so that its bottom is touching the fat. Fat lamps are a great outdoor heat source but should not be used indoors for extended periods of time. *Note:* This same design can be used with gasoline instead of tallow by simply pouring a small amount of fuel over the sand and allowing the bottom side of the wick to slightly penetrate it.

Paraffin Stove

A paraffin stove can be created from corrugated cardboard, paraffin, and an empty tuna can. To make it, cut corrugated cardboard in strips that are approximately 1-inch wide, roll them together, and set them inside the tuna can. Try to pack them inside the can as tightly as possible. Using a double boiler technique melt the paraffin. *Caution:* Paraffin is extremely flammable

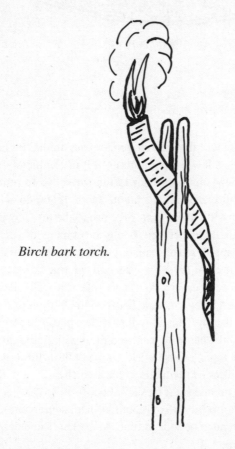

Birch bark torch.

and should never be melted over direct heat. Slowly pour the liquid over the cardboard and into the tuna can (a little goes a long way). Let it cool. If the lid is still attached, it can be used as a cover. Although placing a cotton wick in the center of the cardboard makes lighting easier, it isn't necessary. To use, simply light the cardboard. A paraffin stove can be used for warmth and to cook. If used to prepare food, simply place it under an improvised cooking platform.

TORCHES

Birch Bark Torch
Birch bark is excellent tinder that lights when wet. To make a birch torch, gather up long 2-inch-wide strips of birch and a green sapling that is about 3 feet long. Fold the bark strips in half—lengthwise. Split and trim the end of the sapling so that the bark can slide through it but not so much that it won't be held in place. To use, light the bark and as it burns down feed the fresh bark forward. Another method of using birch as a torch is to simply wrap and tie it around the end of a sapling. This method is wasteful and I don't prefer it.

Cattail Torch
A cattail can provide an excellent torch with its built-in handle and medium for holding fuel. To make, cut the stalk 3 feet from the cattail's head and dip the head into tallow or another fuel source. To use, simply light the head.

6

Water Procurement in the Wild

The faucet provides us with an unending supply of purified water. Where does it come from?

> *The first day in the desert was easy. I made shade shelters and put out several transpiration bags and solar stills. The remainder of the day I rested. On day two I began to worry about my water supply. Although the transpiration bags and solar stills provided some water, it wasn't enough. By the time I finally began looking for an alternative source, I had already developed a headache and become slightly nauseated. Watching the morning flight pattern of the local birds led me up a 200-foot cliff to a small pond. I'll never forget how good it felt to see the stagnant, algae-filled pool. I was drained, however, and it took me several days to recuperate. That trip left me with a heightened respect for how important water is for sustaining my mental alertness, and my life.*

IMPORTANCE OF WATER

Water is far more important than food. You can live anywhere from 3 weeks to 2 months without food but only days without water. Thus, any primitive living site you select must have an accessible water source. After all, if you look at the earth's surface you'll notice—where there is water there is life and where there is no water, life is scarce.

Our bodies are composed of approximately 60 percent water and it plays a vital role in our ability to get through a day. Looking at this in more detail shows that our brains are composed of about 70 percent water, our blood is 82 percent and our lungs are around 90 percent water. In our bloodstream water helps metabolize and transport vital elements, carbohydrates, and proteins that are necessary to fuel our bodies. On the flip side, water helps us dispose of our bodily waste. It's hard to understand why so many people drink so little water.

TYPES OF WATER

SURFACE WATER

Surface water is obtained from rivers, ponds, lakes, streams, etc. It is usually easy to access but is prone to contamination from viruses and *Giardia* and should always be treated. In addition, it is affected by rains and ground movements and may require you to filter it before use. If you build your home site close to surface water, be sure to consider how high it rises during any rainy season or in the spring. It would be a shame to flood out your home.

Collecting water from a stream.

GROUND WATER

Ground water is found under the earth's surface. This water is naturally filtered as it moves through the ground and into underground reservoirs (aquifers). Although treatment may not be necessary, always err on the side of caution when in doubt. The biggest problem with ground water is accessing it.

FINDING WATER (INDICATORS)

INSECTS

If bees are present, water is usually within several miles of your location. Ants require water and will often place their nest close to a source. Swarms of mosquitoes and flies are a good indicator that water is close.

BIRDS

Birds frequently fly toward water at dawn and dusk in a direct, low flight path. This is especially true of birds that feed on grain, such as pigeons and finches. Flesh-eating birds can also be seen exhibiting this flight pattern, but their need for water isn't as great, and they don't require as many trips to the water source. Birds observed circling high in the air during the day are often doing it over water, as well.

FROGS AND SALAMANDERS

Most frogs and salamanders require water and if found are usually a good indicator that water is near.

MAMMALS

Like birds, mammals will frequently visit watering holes at dawn and dusk. This is especially true of mammals that eat a grain or grassy-type diet. Watching their travel patterns or evaluating mammal trails may help you find a water source. Trails that merge into one are usually a good pointer and following the merged trail often leads to water.

LAND FEATURES THAT INDICATE WATER

Drainages and valleys are a good water indicator, as are winding trails of deciduous trees. Green plush vegetation found at the base of a cliff or mountain may indicate a natural spring or underground source of water.

DOWSING

Dowsing, or witching, is a highly debated skill that some say helps them find water. Those who profess to have this skill use a forked stick (shaped like a Y) about 18 to 20 inches long and ⅛ to ¼ inch in diameter. The most common branch used comes from a willow tree. The two ends of the Y are held in the hands, which are positioned palms up, while the dowser walks forward. The free end of the stick is supposed to react when it passes over water. This reaction may be toward or away from the body.

METHODS OF WATER PROCUREMENT

SURFACE WATER

If using surface water, in most situations you should be able to walk to your water source. The water, however, may not always be easy to access or may not be palatable. You may desire to create a seepage basin well to filter out some of the stagnant flavor and provide ease of access. This filtering process is similar to what happens as groundwater moves toward the aquifer. To create this seepage basin well, dig a 3-foot-wide hole about 10 feet from your water source. Dig it down until water begins to seep in and then go about another foot. At this point I usually line the sides with wood or rocks (so that no more mud will fall in) and let it sit overnight. You can use this same process when your home is next to the ocean by simply digging a hole, one dune beyond the beach (inland). As with the other basin wells, dig until water is hit and then line the sides before letting it sit overnight.

GROUND WATER

In a primitive setting it is doubtful that you will have the ability to access water that is located 100 feet below ground. When referring to groundwater, I am talking about the water that is either directly under the surface or is a natural spring that pushes the water up to the surface. Locating groundwater is probably the most difficult part of accessing it. Look for things that seem out of place, such as a small area of green plush vegetation (at the base of a hill) that is surrounded by brown sagebrush. A marshy area with a fair amount of cattail or hemlock growth may provide a clue that groundwater is available. I have found natural springs in desert areas and running water less than 6 feet below the earth's surface by using these very clues. If you decide to use groundwater make sure the source you choose continually replenishes itself. For ease of access, I prefer to dig a small well at the source. As always, I will line the well with wood or rocks and let it sit overnight before I begin to use the water.

WATER FILTRATION SYSTEMS

Filtration systems do not purify water! At best, they remove unwanted particles and make the water more palatable. A seepage basin is one method of filtering water (see above for details). It may not always, however, take away the water's awful taste. Another method is to use a layered filtering device that uses grass, sand, and charcoal. Running water through grass, sand, and black charcoal does more then just remove unwanted particles; it

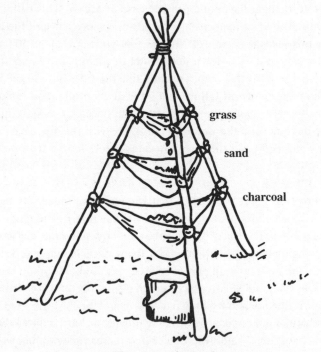

Three-tiered tripod.

also makes the water taste better. This system can be created using a three-tiered tripod design or by simply layering the material inside a container that allows the water passage. I have seen large coffee cans used in the latter design. For a three-tiered tripod, tie three sections of porous material about 1 foot apart and fill each with grass, sand, and charcoal from top to bottom respectively. To use, simply pour the water into the top and catch it as it departs the bottom section.

PURIFYING WATER
There are two basic methods of long-term and ongoing water disinfection: boiling and chemical treatment.

BOILING
The Office of Water of the Environmental Protection Agency (EPA) advocates using a vigorous boil for 1 minute to kill any disease-causing microorganisms in water. My rational mind tells me that this must be based on science and should work. After seeing one of my friends lose about 40 pounds from a severe case of giardiasis, however, I tend to overboil my water. As a general rule, I almost always boil it for around 10 minutes. I'll let you decide what is right for you. Boiling is far superior to chemical treatments and should be done whenever possible.

CHEMICAL TREATMENT
When unable to boil your water, you may elect to use chlorine or iodine. These chemicals are somewhat effective against *Giardia,* but according to the EPA there is some question about their ability to protect you against *Cryptosporidium.* In fact, the EPA advises against using chemicals to purify surface water. This may be unpractical in a wilderness-living setting. Chlorine is preferred over iodine since it seems to offer better protection against *Giardia.* Both chlorine and iodine tend to be less effective in cold water.

Household Chlorine Bleach
The amount of chlorine to use for purifying water will depend upon the amount of available chlorine in the solution. This can usually be found on the label.

PERCENTAGE OF AVAILABLE CHLORINE	DROPS PER QUART OF CLEAR WATER
1	10
4-6	2
7-10	1
Unknown	10

If the water is cloudy or colored, double the normal amount of bleach required for the percentage used. The treated water should be mixed and allowed to stand for 30 minutes before you drink it.

Iodine

There are two types of iodine that are commonly used to treat water, tincture and tablets. The tincture is nothing more than the common household iodine that you may have in your medical kit. This product is usually a 2 percent iodine solution and when used you'll need to add 5 drops to each quart of water. For cloudy water the amount is doubled. The treated water should be mixed and allowed to stand for 30 minutes before being used. If using iodine tablets you should place one tablet in each quart of water when it is warm and two tablets per quart when the water is cold or cloudy. Each bottle of iodine tablets should have the particulars for how it should be mixed and how long you should wait before drinking the water. If no directions are available, usually wait 3 minutes and then vigorously shake the water with the cap slightly loose (allowing some water to weep out through the seams). Then seal the cap on the container and wait another 25 to 30 minutes before loosening the cap and shaking it again. At this point consider the water safe to consume.

7

Food: Understanding Your Options

Using our hard-earned money, we purchase the food that fuels our body, never understanding where it comes from or how it is procured—what would we do if the stores no longer existed?

> *The first 22-day trip I took to the woods I lost 25 pounds. The head-high snow and harsh weather drained my energy and left me feeling weak. The demands of my training along with a limited food supply showed me how harsh living in Mother Nature could be. I drank pine needle tea and ate the meaty cambium found between a tree's bark and inner wood. I longed for a pizza or burger. After several days of this I realized that I controlled my destiny and if I wanted the valuable nutrients nature could provide I'd have to pay closer attention to the vegetation, bugs, and animals around me. When I finally snared a squirrel it not only provided me with a welcome meal but also lifted my spirits about my ability to survive.*

NEED FOR FOOD

One of the biggest problems with long-term survival is meeting your nutritional requirements. Many backcountry enthusiasts focus on meat as their main source of food and often overlook all the other supplies Mother Nature has to provide. The ideal diet has five basic food groups:

1. Carbohydrates: easily digested food that provides rapid energy; most often found in fruits, vegetables, and whole grains.

2. Fats: slowly digested food that provides long lasting energy that is normally utilized once the carbohydrates are gone; most often found in butter, cheese, oils, nuts, eggs, and animal fats. In cold environments it isn't uncommon for the natives to eat fats before bed, believing they will help keep them warm throughout the night.

3. Protein: helps with the building of body cells; most often found in fish, meat, poultry, and blood.

4. Vitamins: provide no calories but aid in the body's daily function and growth. Vitamins occur in most foods and when you maintain a well-balanced diet you will rarely become depleted.

5. Minerals: provide no calories but aid with building and repairing the skeletal system and regulating the body's normal growth. Like vitamins these needs are met when a well-balanced diet is followed. In addition to food, minerals are often present in our water.

The five major food groups and a sixth "use sparingly group" make up your basic dietary regimen:

- Fats, oils, and sweets—use sparingly.
- Milk and cheese group—two to three servings a day.
- Meat, poultry, fish, dry beans, eggs, and nuts group—two to three servings a day.
- Vegetable group—three to five servings a day.
- Fruit group—two to four servings a day.
- Bread, cereal, rice, and pasta group—six to eleven servings a day.

No one group is more important than the other—you need them all for good health. A healthy diet begins with plenty of grains, generous amounts of vegetables and fruits, and a smaller amount of meats and dairy products.

PLANT FOODS

It has been said that over 300,000 species of plants can be found on the earth's surface. With this in mind, it seems logical that plants can provide a major source of your diet. In my backyard, located in Northwest Washington, I can find plantain, dock, miner's lettuce, trillium, queen's cup, pine needles, thistle, nettles, dandelion, grasses, clover, raspberry, blackberry, and wild strawberry. However, I also have water hemlock, a very poisonous plant. Knowing whether a plant is edible can be the difference between life and death. The best way to learn if a plant is edible or not is from those who are indigenous to the area along with a good plant reference book. Be careful, however, and always positively identify a plant before eating it. If you don't have any references and need to establish the edibility of a plant then I'd suggest using the universal edibility test.

UNIVERSAL EDIBILITY TEST

General Rules of the Edibility Test
- Insure there is an abundant supply of the plant.
- Use only fresh vegetation.
- Always wash your plants with treated water.
- Only perform the test on one plant/plant part at a time.
- During the test, don't consume anything other than purified water.
- Don't eat 8 hours prior to starting the test.

Identifying Characteristics of Plants to Avoid
(General Guidelines—There Are Exceptions)
- Mushrooms or mushroomlike appearance.
- Umbrella-shaped flower clusters (resembling parsley, parsnip, or dill).
- Plants with milky sap or sap that turns black when exposed to the air.
- Bulbs (resembling onion or garlic).
- Carrotlike leaves, roots, or tubers.
- Bean- and pealike appearance.
- Plants with fungal infection (common in spoiled plants procured off the ground).
- Plants with shiny leaves or fine hairs.

To Test a Plant
- Break the plant into its basic components: leaves, stems, roots, buds, and flowers.
- Test only one part of the potential food source at a time.
- Smell the plant for strong or acidlike odors. If present, it may be best to select another plant.

**Mushrooms or
mushroomlike
appearance**

**Umbrella-shaped
flower clusters**

**Bulbs resembling
onion or garlic**

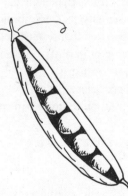

**Carrotlike leaves,
roots, or tubers**

**Bean- and pealike
appearance**

**Plants with shiny
leaves or fine hairs**

Six characteristics of plants to avoid.

- Prepare the plant part in the fashion in which you intend to consume it (raw, boiled, baked and so forth).
- Place a piece of the plant part being tested on the inside of your wrist for 15 minutes. Monitor for burning, stinging, or irritation. If any of these occur, discontinue the test, select another plant (or another component of the one testing), and start over.
- Hold a small portion (about a teaspoonful) of the plant to your lips and monitor for 5 minutes. If any burning or irritation occurs, discontinue the test, select another plant (or another component of the one testing), and start over.
- Place the plant on your tongue, holding it there for 15 minutes. Do not swallow any of the plant juices. If any burning or irritation occurs, discontinue the test, select another plant (or another component of the one testing), and start over.
- Thoroughly chew the teaspoon portion of the plant part for 15 minutes. Do not swallow any of the plant or its juices. If you experience a reaction, discontinue the test, select another plant (or another component of the one testing), and start over. If there is no burning, stinging, or irritation, swallow the plant.
- Wait 8 hours. Monitor for cramps, nausea, vomiting, or other abdominal irritations. If any occur, induce vomiting and drink plenty of water. If you do experience a reaction, discontinue the test, select another plant (or another component of the one testing), and start over.
- If no problems are experienced, eat ½ cup of the plant, prepared in the same fashion as before. Wait another 8 hours. If no ill effects occur, the plant part is edible when prepared in the same fashion as tested.
- Test all parts of the plant you intend to use. Some plants have both edible and poisonous sections. Do not assume that a part that is edible when cooked is edible when raw (or visa versa). Always eat the plant in the same fashion in which the edibility test was performed on it.
- After the plant is determined to be edible, eat it in moderation. Although considered safe, large amounts may cause cramps and diarrhea.

The Berry Rule
In general, the edibility of berries can be classified according to their color and composition. The following is a guideline (approximation) to help you

Aggregate berries are 99 percent edible.

determine if a berry is poisonous. In no way should the berry rule replace the edibility test. Use it as a general guide to determine whether the edibility test needs to be performed upon the berry. The only berries that should be eaten without testing are those that you can positively identify as nonpoisonous.

- Green, yellow, and white berries are 10 percent edible.
- Red berries are 50 percent edible.
- Purple, blue, and black berries are 90 percent edible.
- Aggregate berries such as thimbleberries, raspberries, and blackberries are considered 99 percent edible.

EDIBLE PARTS OF A PLANT
Some plants are completely edible whereas others have both edible and poisonous parts. Unless you have performed the edibility test on the whole plant—only eat the parts that you know are edible. A plant can be broken down into several distinct components (underground; stems and leaves; flowers, fruits, nuts, and seeds; and grains). In addition, some plants provide gums, resins, and saps that are edible.

Underground (Tubers, Roots and Rootstocks, and Bulbs)

Found underground these plant parts have a high degree of starch and are best served baked or boiled. Some examples of these are potatoes (tuber), cattail (root and rootstock), and wild onion (bulbs).

Stems and Leaves (Shoots/Stems, Leaves, Pith, and Cambium)

Plants that produce stems and leaves are probably the most abundant source of edible vegetation in the world. Their high vitamin content makes them a valuable component of our daily diet.

Shoots grow like asparagus and are best when parboiled (boiled five minutes, drained off, and boiled again until done). Some examples are bracken fern (only to be eaten in moderation), young bamboo, and cattail. Leaves may be eaten raw or cooked but they provide the highest nutritional value when eaten raw. Dock, plantain, amaranth, and sorrel are a few examples of edible leaves. Pith, found inside the stem of some plants, is often very high in food value. Some examples are sago, rattan, coconut, and sugar. Cambium is the inner layer found between the bark and the wood of a tree. It can be eaten raw, cooked, or dried and then pulverized into flour.

Flowers (Flowers, Buds, and Pollens)

Flowers, buds, and pollens are high in food value and are best when eaten raw or in a salad. Some examples include hibiscus (flower), rose hips (buds), and cattail (pollen).

Fruits (Sweet and Nonsweet)

Fruits are the seed-bearing part of a plant and can be found in all areas of the world. Best when eaten raw (retaining all their nutritional value), they may also be cooked. Examples of sweet fruits are apples, prickly pears, huckleberries, and wild strawberries. Examples of nonsweet fruits include tomatoes, cucumbers, plantains, and horseradishes.

Nuts

Nuts are high in fat and protein and can be found around the whole world. Most can be eaten raw but some, like acorns, require leaching with several changes of water to remove their tannic acid content.

Seeds and Grains

The seeds and grains of many plants—such as grasses and millet—are a valuable food resource and should not be overlooked. They are best eaten when ground into flour or roasted.

Gums and Resins

Gums and resins are sap that collects on the outside of trees and plants. Their high nutritional value makes them a great augmentation to any meal. Examples can be found on pine and maple trees.

Plants are an abundant food source that should be a major part of your daily diet. If you don't know if it's edible, however, don't eat it without either positively identifying it or performing an edibility test on one or all of its various parts. Become familiar with plants indigenous to your area.

Caution: If unable to identify a plant DO NOT eat it without first performing the edibility test.

BUGS AS A FOOD SOURCE

Many cultures around the world eat bugs as part of their routine diet. An example of this is the pan-fried locusts that are still considered a delicacy in Algeria and several Mexican states. Another example can be found in Malaysia where bee larva is considered a special treat. Our phobia about eating bugs is unfortunate since they provide ample amounts of protein, fats, carbohydrates, calcium, and iron. In addition, comparing bugs with cattle, sheep, pigs, and chickens shows they are far more cost-effective to raise and have far fewer harmful effects related to their rearing. Although

The FDA allows 13 insect heads in 100 grams of fig paste.

bugs are not harvested for food in the United States, those of us who purchase our foods at the store are eating them every day. The Food and Drug
Administration (FDA) allows certain levels of bugs to be present in various
foods. The accepted standards are for up to 60 aphids in 3½ ounces of
broccoli, 2 to 3 fruit fly maggots in 200 grams of tomato juice, 100 insect
fragments in 25 grams of curry powder, 74 mites in 100 grams of canned
mushrooms, 13 insect heads in 100 grams of fig paste, and 34 fruit fly eggs
in every cup of raisins.

A study done by Jared Ostrem and John VanDyk for the Entomology
Department of Iowa State University—comparing lean ground beef and
fish with certain bugs—showed the following results:

NUTRITIONAL VALUE OF VARIOUS INSECTS
(PER 100 GRAMS)

	Protein (g)	Fats (g)	Carbohydrates (g)	Calcium (mg)	Iron (mg)
Crickets	12.9	5.5	5.1	75.8	9.5
Small grasshoppers	20.6	6.1	3.9	35.2	5
Giant water beetles	19.8	8.3	2.1	43.5	13.6
Red ants	13.9	3.5	2.9	47.8	5.7
Silkworm pupae	9.6	5.6	2.3	41.7	1.8
Termites	14.2			0.050	35.5
Weevils	6.7			0.186	13.1
For Comparison					
Lean ground beef	24.0	18.3	0	9.0	2.09
Fish broiled cod	22.95	0.86	0	0.031	1.0

Bugs can be found throughout the world and they are easy to procure. In
addition, the larvae or grubs of many are edible and easily found in rotten

logs, underground, or under the bark of dead trees. Although a fair number of bugs can be eaten raw, it is best to cook them in order to avoid the ingestion of unwanted parasites. As a general rule, avoid bugs that carry disease (flies, mosquitoes, and ticks), poisonous insects (centipedes and spiders), and bugs that have fine hair, bright colors, and eight or more legs.

CRUSTACEANS
Freshwater and saltwater crabs, crayfish, lobster, shrimp, and prawns are all forms of crustaceans. Although all are edible, it is important to cook freshwater crustaceans, as many carry parasites.

FRESHWATER SHRIMP
Freshwater shrimp are abundant in most tropical streams, especially where the water is sluggish. They can be seen swimming or clinging to branches and are easily procured by using either a scoop net or your hand.

SALTWATER SHRIMP
Saltwater shrimp live on or near the sea bottom. Since these shrimp are attracted to light, it's best to hunt them during a full moon or to lure them to the water's surface with a flashlight. Once spotted, simply scoop them up with a net or pluck them from the water with your hand.

FRESHWATER CRABS AND CRAYFISH
Freshwater crabs and crayfish are found on moss beds, under rocks and brush at the bottom of streams, or swimming in the stream's shallow water. Since they are nocturnal, they are easier to spot at night and then catch by hand or with a scoop net. To catch during the day, use a lobster trap or baited hook. A improvised lobster trap can be made by securely placing bait to the inside bottom of a container (improvised or man-made) that is the size of a large coffee can. If using a can, be sure to puncture small holes into the bottom so that water can pass through it. Attach enough line to the trap's sides so that it can be lowered and raised from the stream's bottom. Once the trap is placed, it won't take long before the crab or crayfish crawls inside to eat the bait. Thus, it should be checked often. When pulling the container from the water, do it swiftly but with enough control to avoid pouring your dinner out.

SALTWATER CRAYFISH AND LOBSTER
Saltwater crayfish and lobster are found on the ocean bottoms in 10 to 30 feet of water. These crustaceans behave similar to the freshwater crabs and crayfish and can be procured using the same techniques described for them.

MOLLUSKS

If you are located near water, mollusks can provide an almost never-ending food source. They should, however, be avoided from April to October. During this time, they accumulate certain poisons that can be harmful to humans. The most common types of mollusks are freshwater and saltwater shellfish—bivalves, river snails, freshwater periwinkles, mussels, snails, limpets, and chitons. All can be boiled, steamed, or baked.

BIVALVES, RIVER SNAILS, AND FRESHWATER PERIWINKLES
Bivalves, river snails, and periwinkles are all freshwater mollusks and are easily procured. Bivalves are found worldwide under all water conditions. River snails and freshwater periwinkles are most plentiful in the rivers, streams, and lakes of the northern coniferous forests.

MUSSELS, CHITONS, SEA SNAILS, AND LIMPETS
Mussels, chitons, sea snails, and limpets are all saltwater mollusks and are easily procured at low tide. All can be found in dense colonies on rocks and logs above the surf line. *Note:* Avoid shellfish that are not covered by water at high tide.

REPTILES

Lizards, snakes, and turtles are all forms of reptiles. Although alligators are edible, I choose to leave them alone.

LIZARDS
Although lizards can be found almost anywhere, they are abundant in the tropics and subtropics. There are only two that are poisonous and they can only be found in the American Southwest, Mexico, and Central America. All are edible. Lizards can be caught with a noose on the end of a stick or stunned and killed with a club or rock. To prepare lizards, skin them and broil or fry the meat.

SNAKES

All poisonous and nonpoisonous freshwater and land snakes are edible and can be located almost anywhere there is cover. For best results hunt for snakes in the early morning or evening hours. Always be cautious when dealing with poisonous snakes.

To catch or kill snakes use a long stick that has a fork on one end. After stunning the snake with a thrown rock or stick, use the forked end of the stick to pin its head to the ground. Kill it with a rock, knife, or another stick (be careful). Snakes can be cooked in any fashion but all should be skinned and gutted. To skin a snake, sever its head (avoid accidental poisoning by burying the head) and peel back its skin until you can grab it and pull it down (inside out) the length of the snake. If you can't pull it free, then make a cut down the length of the snake to help you free the skin. The entrails will usually come out during this process but, if not, grabbing them at the top and pulling them down will remove them.

TURTLES

Turtles are found throughout the temperate and tropic regions of the world almost anywhere there is water. Marine, freshwater, and land turtles are all edible. The smaller turtles can be clubbed or perhaps caught with fishing line. To cook the turtle, you'll need to remove the shell. This can be done from its belly side. Cook in any fashion desired. Don't discard the shell as it will provide for many improvising needs.

FISH

Fish are commonly found in almost all sources of water. The best time to fish is just before dawn or just after dusk, at night when the moon is full, and when bad weather is imminent. Fish tend to be close to banks and shallow water in the morning and evening hours. In addition, fish can be found in calm deep pools (especially where transitions from ripples to calm or calm to ripples occur); under outcroppings and overhanging undercuts, brush, or logs; in eddies below rocks or logs; and at the mouth of an intersection with another stream. Avoid fish that have slimy bodies, bad odor, suspicious color (gills should be pink and scales pronounced), and/or flesh that remains indented after being pressed.

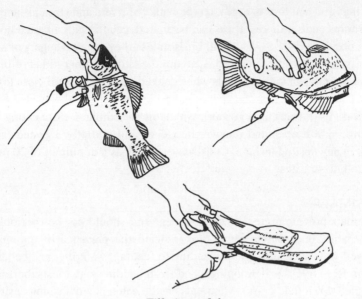

Filleting a fish.

Some methods of fish procurement include fishing tackle, gill nets, spears, poisons, and even your bare hands. To prevent spoilage, prepare the fish as soon as possible. Gut the fish by cutting upward on its abdomen and then removing the intestines and large blood vessels (kidney) that lie next to the backbone. Remove the gills and when applicable, scale and/or skin the fish. On bigger fish you may want to fillet the meat off the bone. To do this, cut behind the fish's gill plates on each side of its head and slide the knife under the meat next to the backbone. Keeping the knife firmly placed against the backbone, begin slicing toward the tail. Next, hold the tail's skin and slide the knife between the skin and meat, cutting forward using a slight sawing motion.

BIRDS

Almost all birds are edible. If nests are near, eggs may also be available for consumption. Birds are commonly found at the edge of the woods where clearings end and forests begin, on the banks of rivers and streams, and on lakeshores and seashores. Birds can be snared, caught with a baited hook, or on occasion clubbed. Pluck all birds unless they are scavengers or sea-birds, which should be skinned. Leaving the skin on other kinds of birds will retain more of their nutrients when cooked. Cut the neck off close to the body. Cut open the chest and abdominal cavity and remove the insides. Save the neck, liver, heart, and gizzard, which all are edible. Before eating the gizzard, split it open and remove the stones and partially digested food. Cook in any desired fashion. Cook scavenger birds a minimum of 20 minutes to kill parasites.

MAMMALS

Mammals provide a great source of meat and should not be overlooked as a viable food source. Signs that indicate the presence of mammals are well-traveled trails (usually leading to feeding, watering, and bedding areas), fresh tracks and droppings, and fresh bedding sign (nests, burrows, trampled-down field grass). Mammals can be eaten in any fashion desired. To eat you'll need to skin, gut, and butcher most game. Skinning an animal is covered in chapter 2.

To gut an animal, place the carcass, belly up, on a slope or hang it from a tree by its hind legs. Make a small incision just in front of the anus, and insert your index and middle finger into the cut, spreading them apart to form a V. Slide the knife into the incision between the V formed by your two fingers. Use your fingers to push the internal organs down (away from the knife) and as a guide for the knife as you cut the abdominal cavity upward to the breastbone (avoid cutting the bladder/internal organs). Cut around the anus and sex organs so that they will be easily removed with the entrails. If the bladder or internal organs are punctured, wash the meat as soon as possible.

Remove the intact bladder by pinching it off close to the opening and cutting it free. Remove the entrails, pulling them down and away from the carcass. To do this you will need to sever the intestines at the anus. Save the liver and kidneys for later consumption. *Note:* If the liver is spotted, a sign of disease, discard all internal organs and thoroughly cook the meat. Cut through the diaphragm and reach inside the chest cavity until you can touch the windpipe. Cut or pull the windpipe free and remove the chest

Dressing a rabbit without a knife.

cavity contents. Save the lungs and heart for later consumption. *Note:* All internal organs can be cooked in any fashion but are best when used in a stew.

Small game like rabbits can be dressed without a knife and the hair singed off in a fire. To do this, firmly grasp the rabbit between both hands at its rib cage and squeeze toward the stomach. Using a firm grip, raise the rabbit over your head and fling it down hard (allow your arms to go between your legs) causing the entrails to be expelled.

If you intend to eat the liver, you'll need to remove the small black sac (gallbladder), as it's not edible. If it breaks, wash the liver immediately to avoid tainting the meat. Since fat spoils quickly, it should be cut away from the meat and promptly utilized (best in soups). Cut the legs, back, and breast sections free of one another to easily butcher small game. When you are butchering large game, cut it into meal-sized roasts and steaks that can be stored for later use. Cut the rest of the meat along the grain into long, thin strips about ⅛-inch thick, to be preserved by smoking or sun drying (covered in chapter 11). Don't forget the head: the meat, tongue, eyes, and brain are all edible, as is the marrow inside bones. Keep the bones, brain, sinew, hoofs, and other parts. Each will serve many different survival needs.

8

Passive Food Procurement

What if there were no stores and you didn't have the time to hunt?

> *I set out multiple snares and hoped to catch at least one squirrel. The instructor had showed me the basics and now it was my turn to show him I'd listened. There were several active holes and at least two feeding areas with a lot of pine midden. It was obvious that the squirrels were eating well. The best part about using snares is that I was able to go about meeting my needs while they worked for me. When I finally snared a squirrel, I brought it into the well-established camp I had created while the snares were busy procuring my dinner.*

FISHING TACKLE

The world is covered with water and fish as a food source should not be overlooked. What if you don't have any fishing line or hooks, however? The answer is simple; you'll need to improvise. The crude tackle isn't very useful for catching small fish like trout but has proven somewhat effective with larger fish like carp, catfish, and whitefish. Hooks are best made from bone or wood and the ideal material for improvised fishing line is stinging nettle, milkweed, or dogbane that is braided (covered in chapter 12) into a 10-foot section. Sinew is another option but when it gets wet it tends to stretch and its knots like to loosen. The three most commonly used improvised hooks are the skewer, cross hook, and barbed thorn or branch.

SKEWER HOOK

A skewer hook is a sliver of bone or wood that is notched and tied at the middle. When baited this hook is turned parallel to the line making it easier for the fish to swallow. Once the fish takes the bait, a simple tug on the line will turn the skewer sideways lodging it in its mouth.

CROSS HOOK

A cross hook is made by attaching a crosspiece to a main shank so that when the bait is applied the two pieces are parallel to one another. When the fish swallows the hook, a gentle tug on the line will set it by causing the crosspiece to angle out.

BARBED THORN OR BRANCH HOOK

A barbed thorn or branch hook requires minimal effort to create. Using a branch or thorn that provides a hooklike fork, simply cut a circular notch on one end (for the line) and sharpen the other.

To attach your hook to your braided line, use the following method:

- Notch the hook shank at either its center or distal end (depending on the type of hook you are using).
- Smear it with pitch or other glue-type substance.
- Wrap and tie your improvised line tightly around the notch.
- Seal the line and notch area with additional pitch.

Although you could attach this line to a single pole, I'd advise setting out multiple lines. This method allows you to catch fish while attending to other chores. The goal is to return and find a fish attached to the end of each line.

Three improvised hooks.

GILL NET

The gill net is a very effective method of procuring fish. As with setting lines, it will work for you while you attend to other needs. This makes it an excellent choice. If you have parachute cord or similar material, its inner core provides an ideal material for making a net. Other options are braided stinging nettle, milkweed, and dogbane line. In order for the net to stay clear of debris, it should be placed at a slight angle to the current using stones to anchor the bottom and wood to help the top float. To make a gill net:

• Tie a piece of line between two trees at eye height. The bigger the net you want, the farther apart the trees should be.

• Using a girth hitch, tie the center of your inner core line or other material to the upper cord (use an even number of lines). Be sure to space each line at a distance equal to the width you desire for your net's mesh. For creeks and small rivers, 1 inch is about right.

• No matter which side you start on, skip the line closest to the tree. Tie the second and third together with an overhand knot and continue on down the line tying the fourth and fifth, sixth and seventh, and so on together. When you reach the end there should be one line left.

• Moving in the opposite direction, tie the first line to the second, third to the fourth, and so on. When you reach the end there shouldn't be any lines left.

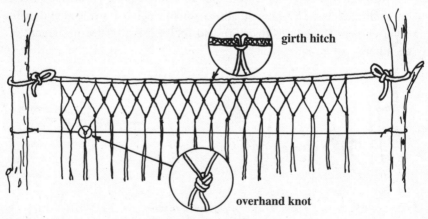

Constructing a gill net.

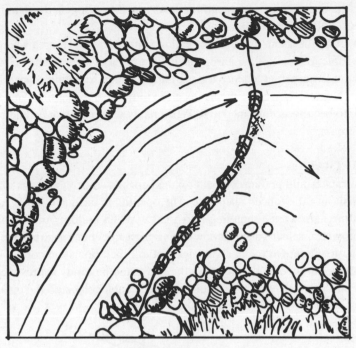

Gill net placement.

- Repeat the last two steps until done.
- If overly concerned about the mesh size, tie a guideline between the two trees. For a 1-inch mesh tie the line 1 inch below the top and use it to determine where the overhand knots should be placed. Once a line is completed it is moved down another inch and so on.
- When done, run parachute line or other material along the net's sides and bottom to help stabilize it.

SCOOP NET

To make a scoop net, procure a 6-foot sapling and bend the two ends together to form a circle. You can also use a forked branch by forming a circle with the forked ends. Allow some extra length for a handle. Lash the ends together. The net's mesh can be made in the same method as described for building a gill net by tying the initial girth hitch to the sapling. Once you have the appropriate size, tie all the lines together using an overhand knot and trim off any excess line.

As with the spear, use a net in shallow water or a similar area where fish are visible. Because of the difference in light refraction above and below the water, it is important to place the net into the water to obtain proper alignment. Next, slowly move the net as close to the fish as possible and allow them to become accustomed to it. When ready scoop the fish up and out of the stream.

FISH TRAPS

Fish traps would perhaps be better called corrals since the idea is to herd the fish into the fenced enclosure. The opening is designed like a funnel with the narrow end emptying into a cage. When building these traps in ocean water, select your location during high tide and construct the trap during low tide. On rocky shores use natural rock pools, on coral islands use the natural pools that form on the reefs, and on sandy shores create a dam on the lee side of the offshore sandbar. If able, block all the openings

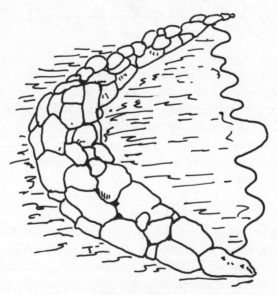

Off-shore fish trap.

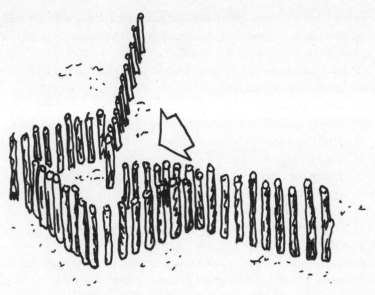

Placement of a fish trap in a creek.

before the tide recedes. Once the tide goes back out you can use either a scoop net or spear to bring your dinner ashore. In creeks and small rivers use saplings to create the trap and its funnel. The opening should be on the upstream side so the current will aid in the funneling process. To herd the fish into your trap, start upstream and wade down toward your corral. Once there, close its opening and use the scoop net or spear the fish.

FISH POISON

Fish poisons are an effective method of procuring food as long as you are prepared to gather the fish as it floats to the surface. In ponds this shouldn't pose a problem but in creeks and rivers it will. You need a net or trap to capture the fish as they float away.

Although these poisons stun the fish, they are not considered harmful to humans. The best known of all fish poisons comes from the derris plant of Southeast Asia. A commercial fish poison called rotenone is derived from this plant. To use the derris plant, crush its root and mix it with water before dropping large amounts of it into the headwater of a slow moving stream or into pools. The water temperature and movement along with the mixture's concentration will dictate the amount of time before the poison takes effect, causing the fish to float to the surface.

Plants that have been said to stun fish—when crushed and added to small pools or slow moving creeks—are:

- Derris plant root.
- Turkey mullein leaves and stalks.
- Buckeye (horse chestnut) seeds/nuts.
- Soap plant root.
- Pokeweed berries.
- Husks of "green" black walnuts.
- Wild cucumber roots.

SNARES AND TRAPS

Snares and traps are highly advantageous because they allow you to meet other needs while still attempting to procure food. The more you place, the better your odds.

METHOD OF CATCHING ANIMALS WITH A SNARE OR TRAP

- Strangle: the animal is caught with a snare that tightens around its neck.
- Mangle: the animal is killed when the snare's trigger is tripped and a log or other device falls on it. Some snares also force the animal into spears when hit by the log.
- Hold: usually a hole or box that holds the animal in place.

SNARE PLACEMENT

When placing a snare, avoid disturbing the area as much as possible. Avoid removing the bark from any natural material used in the snare's construction. If the bark is removed, camouflage the exposed wood by rubbing dirt on it. Since animals avoid humans, it's important to remove your scent from the snare. One method of hiding your scent is to hold the snaring material over smoke or under water for several minutes prior to its final placement.

If establishing a snare on a well-traveled trail, try to utilize the natural funneling of any surrounding vegetation. If natural funneling isn't available, create your own with strategically placed sticks. Again, hide your scent.

The snare's loop (discussed below) should be situated so its height is equal to the height of the animal's head. Secure the snare in place by using one of the triggers/methods discussed below. Place multiple snares at burrow openings and on the well-traveled trails in the area. Be sure to check your snares at dawn and dusk and always make sure any caught game is dead before getting too close.

SNARE TRIGGERS

Toggle Triggers

One-Pin Toggle
The one-pin toggle trigger is primarily used to procure small game in a deadfall-mangling snare.

To construct a one-pin toggle, gather one straight 8- to 12-inch-long branch that can be easily cut in half. Cut across its diameter, creating two pieces that respectively measure one-third and two-thirds of its length. Create a small notch across the center of each branch (on the cut side) so

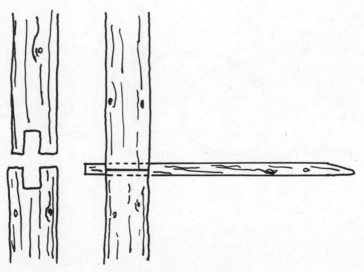

One-pin toggle trigger.

that a small twig can sit between the pieces when they are placed back together. This twig will provide the trigger to the one-pin toggle.

To use the one-pin toggle, place the twig between the two pieces and place it perpendicular to the ground with the longer piece up. Laying a large rock against the upper end of the toggle provides enough weight to arm the trigger and hold it all together. The device is tripped when the twig is moved. This can be facilitated by having it placed in the direct travel pattern of an animal or putting food on the twig.

Two-Pin Toggle
The two-pin toggle trigger is primarily used to procure small game in a strangling snare.

To construct a two-pin toggle, procure two small forked or hooked branches that ideally fit together when the hooks are placed in opposing positions. If unable to find two small forked or hooked branches, construct them by carving notches into two small pieces of wood until they fit together.

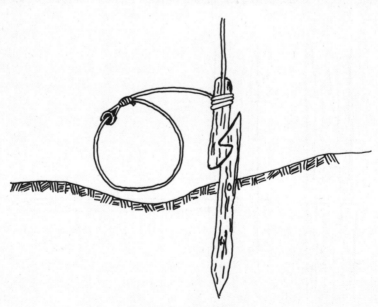

Two-pin toggle trigger.

Three-pin toggle trigger.

To use a two-pin toggle, firmly secure one branch into the ground so that the fork is pointing down. Attach the snare to the second forked branch, which is also tied to a sapling or other device so that when the trigger is tripped, the animal is captured or strangled. To arm the snare, simply bend the sapling and bring the two-pin toggle together. The resultant tension will hold it in place.

Three-Pin Toggle
The three-pin toggle is usually used to hold logs in a mangle-type snare or trap.

To construct a three-pin toggle, tie two 6-inch-long and 1- to 2-inch-diameter pieces of wood to a tree at about mid-leg height for the animal you intend to snare. Space these sticks approximately 2 inches apart. *Note:* Perhaps the tree can provide a similar design when two of its lower branches are cut 2 inches from the bark. A third stick (the trigger) needs to be about 4 inches long and ¾ inches in diameter and should be placed under the two pins.

To use a three-pin toggle trigger, either attach meat to the trigger or run a trip line from it. To hold the trigger under the two other pieces (perpendicular), attach it to a line that will pull it upward when looped over a sturdy branch and secured to a suspended log or other heavy object. This object will fall and mangle an animal that trips the trigger.

Figure Four Triggers

Upright Figure Four
The upright figure four provides an excellent trigger for killing small game with a mangle-type snare or trap.

To construct an upright figure four, procure two sticks that are 12 to 18 inches long and approximately ¾ to 1 inch in diameter (upright and diagonal) and one stick that is the same diameter but 3 to 6 inches longer (trigger). The upright stick is prepared by cutting a 45-degree angle at its top end and creating a squared notch 3 to 4 inches up from the bottom. For best results, cut a diagonal taper from the bottom of the squared notch to the stick's bottom. (Refer to the diagram.) This will aid in the trigger's release from the upright. In addition to being at opposite ends, the bottom's squared notch and the top's 45-degree angle must also be perpendicular to one another.

To create the diagonal piece, cut a diagonal notch 2 inches from one end and a 45-degree angle on the opposite end. In addition to being at opposite ends, the diagonal notch and 45-degree angle must also be on the same side of the stick. The trigger piece needs to have a diagonal notch cut 1 to 2 inches from one end and a squared notch created at the spot where this piece crosses the upright when the three sticks are put together. To determine this location, place the upright perpendicular to the ground and insert its diagonal cut into the notch of the diagonal piece. Put the angled cut of the diagonal stick into the trigger's notch and hold it so that the number four is created between the three sticks when the trigger passes the upright's square notch. Mark the trigger stick and make a squared notch that has a slight diagonal taper from its bottom towards its other notched end. (Refer to diagram.) If you intend to bait the trigger, then make sure to sharpen its free end to a point.

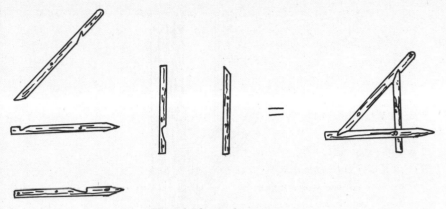

Upright figure four trigger.

To use an upright figure four, put the three pieces together as mentioned and lean a large rock or other weight against the diagonal (at an approximate 45-degree angle to the upright). The entire structure is held in place by the tension that occurs between the weight and the stick's design. This object will fall and mangle an animal that trips the trigger.

Upside Down Figure Four

This figure four design provides the perfect trigger for killing medium to large game with a mangle-type snare or trap.

To construct an upside down figure four, procure two sticks that are 12 inches long and approximately ¾ to 1 inch in diameter (upright and trigger) and one stick that is 4 to 6 inches long and ¾ to 1 inch in diameter (horizontal). Notch the first long stick (upright) 2 inches from one end and cut it at a 45-degree angle at the other. In addition to being at opposite ends, the notch and 45-degree angle must also be on opposite sides of the stick.

In the second long stick (trigger), carve a notch approximately 1 inch from one end and 2 inches from the other. Here the two notches need to be on the same side of the stick and slightly angled away from the stick's center. Sharpen the end—where the notch is 2 inches away—into a point so that it can be used to hold bait when the snare is completed. The short

Upside down figure four trigger.

Bill Frye teaches the proper construction of an upside down figure four trigger while building a mangle trap.

stick (horizontal) should be carved so that both ends have a 45-degree angle, with the angles on the same side of the stick.

To use an upside down figure four, attach the upright to a tree so that the notch is up and the end with the 45-degree angle is down. Be sure the notch points out and the long end of the angled side is away from the tree. Place the trigger onto the upright so that the notch and pointed end are up. It is held in place when the horizontal piece is placed between the trigger and the upright, forming a figure four. The entire structure is held in place by the tension that occurs when the horizontal piece is attached to a line, which ideally loops over a sturdy branch and is secured to a suspended log or other heavy object. This object will fall and mangle an animal that trips the trigger.

Figure H Trigger

The figure H trigger is used to procure small game in a strangling-type snare. If this trigger is used properly, it will work regardless of which way the animal approaches the snare.

To construct a figure H, procure two sticks that are 18 inches long and 1 inch in diameter and one stick that is 8 to 10 inches long and 1 inch in diameter. Notch the two longer sticks approximately 1 inch from the top. Make the notch the same width as the diameter of the shorter stick. Notch the shorter stick, on opposing sides, ½ to 1 inch from its ends. These notches should be the same width as the diameter of the longer sticks.

Figure H trigger.

To use a figure H, pound the two longer sticks into the ground with their carved notches on the up side but in opposing directions. Be sure the notches are the same height from the ground. Place the shorter piece so that its grooves fit into the longer sticks' notches. Attach the snare to the shorter stick, which is also tied to a sapling or other device so that when the trigger is tripped the animal is captured or strangled.

Forked Stick Trigger

The forked stick trigger is used to procure small and large game. If used in a twitch up design, it is ideal for small game; when used in a mangle design, it can release a large rock or log on a medium to large animal.

To construct a forked stick trigger, procure a forked branch (one in which the forked ends are long enough to pound into the ground), a stick (trigger) that easily spans the width of the forked branch plus 6 to 8 inches, and a small third stick (release) that is approximately 2 to 3 inches long. Pound one or both ends of the forked branch into the ground (leaving enough height for the release to clear between it and the ground).

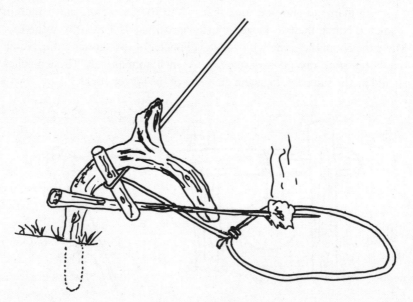

Forked stick trigger.

To use a forked stick trigger, place the trigger on one side of the forked branch and between it and the top of the fork, place the release. The entire structure is held in place by the tension that occurs when the release is attached to a line, which is then either tied to a sapling (twitch up design) or looped over a sturdy branch and secured to a suspended log or other heavy object (mangle design). Depending on your design, when the trigger is released, the device will either catch the animal in a snare or mangle it below a rock or log. If used as a twitch up device, be sure that the loop does not pass under the arch of the forked stick. Keep it on the same side as your sapling.

Spring Release Trigger

The spring release trigger is used to procure medium and large game. It can be used with both a twitch up and mangle design. Small game will usually fail to release the trigger.

To construct a spring release trigger, gather two sticks (with a forked branch at one end) that are 10 inches long and ¾ to 1 inch in diameter, five ¾-to 1-inch-diameter sticks that are about 2 feet long, two ¾-to 1-inch-diameter branches (trigger) that are about 18 inches long, and one stick (release) that is 2 to 3 inches long with a diameter of ½ to ¾ of an inch. Sharpen the far end of the forked branches and pound them securely into the ground (leave about 4 to 5 inches exposed) so that they are 12 to 15 inches apart. Place the two trigger sticks perpendicular to the forked branches and between the forks and the ground. Insert the five longer branches between and perpendicular to the two trigger pieces. These branches should be placed so that about 1 inch extends beyond the forked side of the trigger. The release should be sharpened on one end so that bait can be attached.

To use a spring release trigger, place the release between the two forked branches (from the forked side and at the center point) and perpendicular to the trigger sticks. The sharpened end should face up and can be used to hold bait. The entire structure is held in place by the tension that occurs when the release is attached to a line, which is then either tied to a sapling (twitch up design) or looped over a sturdy branch and secured to a suspended log or other heavy object (mangle design). This line pulls the release into the two trigger sticks by running between them and toward the sapling or log from the opposite side. The trigger is released when an animal steps

Spring release trigger.

on the five long branches (forcing the lower trigger branch down). The device will either catch the animal in a snare (placed over the five branches) or mangle it below a rock or log.

SNARES AND TRAPS

For each of the snares described, proper placement and trigger design is essential for success. Please take the time to review this information before attempting to use any of these devices. A properly used snare will strangle, mangle, or hold your game.

Snares That Strangle

Simple Loop Snare

An animal caught in this type of snare will either strangle itself or be held secure until your arrival. To construct a simple loop snare, use either snare wire or any line (improvised or man-made) that's strong enough to hold the mammal you intend to catch. Regardless of the material you use, start by making a fixed loop at one end. If using snare wire, bend the wire 2 inches

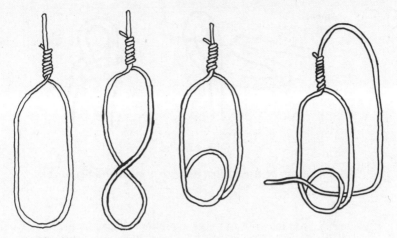

The four steps of constructing a simple loop snare with wire.

from the end, fold it back on itself, and twist or wrap the end of the wire and its body together, being sure to leave a small loop. Twist the fixed loop at its midpoint until it forms a figure eight. Fold the top half of the figure eight down onto the lower half.

Run the free end of the line or wire through the fixed loop. The size of the snare will determine the resultant circle's diameter. It should be slightly larger than the head size of the animal you intend to catch. If used in extremely cold weather, its best to double snare wire in order to prevent the snare from breaking.

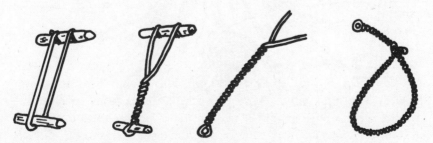

Doubling the line over on itself will increase its overall strength.

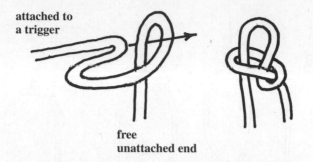

**attached to
a trigger**

**free
unattached end**

A slipknot can be used when a snare is made from cordage.

If using line, you may opt to make a slipknot that tightens down when the animal puts its head through it and lunges forward.

Place the simple loop snare at den openings, well-traveled trails, or other likely spots. Attach the free end to a branch, rock, or drag stick. A drag stick is a big stick that is either too heavy for the animal to drag or gets stuck in the surrounding debris when the animal tries moving.

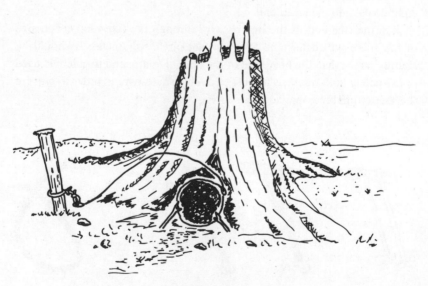

A simple loop snare.

*A squirrel pole is an efficient means by which to catch multiple squirrels
with minimal time, effort, and materials.*

Squirrel Pole

A squirrel pole is an efficient means by which to catch multiple squirrels
with minimal time, effort, or materials. Attach several simple loop snares
(see above) to a pole approximately 6-feet long, then lean the pole onto
an area with multiple squirrel feeding signs—look for mounds of pinecone
scales, usually on a stump or a fallen tree. The squirrel will inevitably use
the pole to try get to his favorite feeding site.

Twitch-up Strangle Snare

An animal caught in this type of snare will either strangle itself or be held
securely until your arrival. The advantage of the twitch-up snare over the
simple loop snare is that it will hold your catch beyond the reach of other
predatory animals that might wander by. To construct a twitch-up strangle
snare, begin by making a simple loop snare out of either snare wire or strong
improvised line. Find a sapling that when bent to 90 degrees is directly over
the snare site you have selected. Using a two-pin toggle, securely insert the
longer forked branch into the ground at the snare site, and with its hook
pointing downward. (Notching a sapling that is located close to the trail or

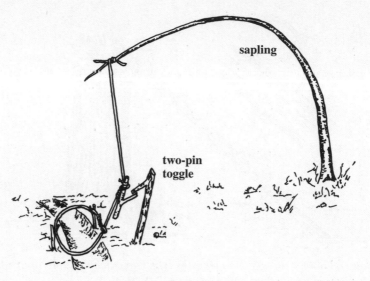

Twitch-up strangle snare.

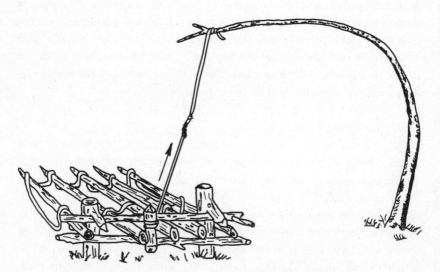

Twitch-up strangle snare using a spring release trigger.

den can also create this piece of the snare.) Attach the free end of the snare wire (created earlier) to the other forked branch. *Note:* Other trigger options include a figure H and forked stick—for small game—and spring release for large game. With a short piece of snare wire, secure the free branch to the sapling, bend the sapling down, and couple the trigger together. The resultant tension will hold the trigger in place. Adjust the snare height to the approximate position of the animal's head. When an animal places its head through the snare and trips the trigger, it will be snapped upward and strangled by the snare. If using improvised line, it may be necessary to place two small sticks into the ground to hold the snare open and in a proper place on the trail. If using a spring release trigger, be sure to cover the trigger and snare line with leaves or similar material.

Snares That Mangle

Figure Four Mangle Snare
The figure four mangle snare is often used to procure small rodents like mice, squirrels, and marmots. An animal caught in this snare will be mangled and killed. To create this mangling snare, use an upright figure four trigger and a large rock (or log). To construct the figure four trigger, place

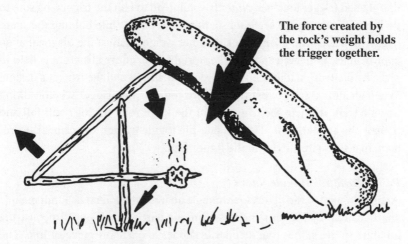

The force created by the rock's weight holds the trigger together.

Figure four mangle snare.

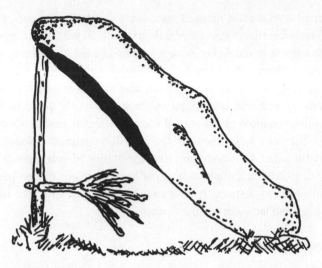

Using a one-pin toggle trigger, you can create a mangle snare similar to the figure four.

the upright perpendicular to the ground, insert its diagonal cut into the notch of the diagonal piece, place the angled end of the diagonal section into the trigger's notch, and tie it all together by placing the square cuts of the upright and trigger together. *Note:* If you intend to bait the trigger, be sure to do it before putting the separate sections together. While holding the snare trigger in place, lean a large rock or other weight against the diagonal at an approximate 45-degree angle to the upright. The entire structure is held in place by the tension that occurs between the weight and the trigger's design. When an animal tries to eat the meat or touches the trigger when walking down a trail, it'll trip the trigger, and the large rock (or log) will fall and mangle the animal. *Note:* Using a one-pin toggle trigger, you can easily create a mangle snare similar to the figure four.

Paiute Deadfall Mangle Snare
Another option to the figure four mangle snare is the Paiute deadfall mangle snare. Its touchy trigger system is a unique part of its design. To construct a Paiute snare, gather four slender branches and a short piece of line. The five parts of this trap are referred to as the upright, diagonal, trigger, bait,

and line. *Note:* The Paiute snare is difficult to explain, so please refer often to the illustration.

- The upright (the only one in contact with the ground) needs to have a flat bottom and beveled top. It should be long enough to create a 45-degree angle between your mangle device (most often a rock) and the ground.
- The diagonal piece is approximately two-thirds the length of the upright. Prepare this piece by cutting a notch on one end (approximately 1 inch from the tip) and a circular groove (½ inch up) around the other end.
- The trigger is a small branch that needs to be long enough to extend 1 inch beyond both sides of the upright when it is placed perpendicular to it.
- The bait stick should be long enough to touch both the trigger stick (when in appropriate position—see below) and the rock when it is held parallel to the ground.
- The line or cordage is attached to the diagonal piece's circular notch and needs to be long enough to wrap around the lower end of the upright while attached to the trigger. Attach the line to the trigger so that it's on the side that ends up opposite of the line coming off the diagonal piece. It should be cut so that when the trap is set, it creates a 45-degree angle between the upper ends of the diagonal and upright piece.

Paiute deadfall trap.

To arm the Paiute snare:

• Tie the line to the circular groove of the diagonal stick.

• Place the diagonal branch (notch side up) on the up side of the rock forming a 45-degree angle between the rock and the ground.

• Put the beveled side of the upright into the notch while maintaining the 45-degree angle. The upright should be placed so it is approximately perpendicular to the ground.

• Run the line (off the diagonal branch's groove) around the upright (the line should already be attached to the trigger) so that the trigger is perpendicular to the upright and on the side away from the rock.

• Hold the trigger in place with the bait stick, which should be placed so that it is parallel to the ground with one end touching the trigger (on the side opposite of the line coming off of the diagonal stick) and the other touching the lower end of the rock.

• Food should be placed on the bait stick prior to arming the trigger. When the rodent tries to eat the food, it will trip the trigger, causing the rock to fall on it.

Fall-Log Mangle Snare

An animal caught in this snare will be mangled and killed by a log or rock that falls when the trigger is released. A three-pin toggle or upside down figure four trigger can be used. To construct a trip line mangle snare (using a three-pin toggle), set the trigger up, as outlined above, approximately 1½ to 2 feet high on a small 1- to 2-foot-wide tree. Attach line and bait to the lower section of the trigger and run the line up and over a strong branch in the tree. Tie the free end of the line 1 foot from the up side end of a heavy, well-positioned log. Well-positioned means it will fall directly on the animal when the trigger is released. The log should be 6 to 8 feet long and form a 25- to 30-degree angle between its high side and its low side and the ground. When an animal takes the bait, it will trip the trigger and the upper end of the log will fall, mangling the animal.

Canadian Ace Mangle Snare

The Canadian ace mangle snare is almost identical to the fall log mangle snare, except that when the trigger releases a log or rock, it drives the animal into sharpened sticks. An animal caught in this snare will be mangled and killed. It's used primarily on larger predatory game, such as coyotes.

*Fall-log
mangle snare.*

*Canadian ace
mangle snare.*

To construct a Canadian ace mangle snare (using an upside down figure four), set the trigger approximately 2 to 3 feet high on a small 1- to 2-foot-wide tree. Gather multiple straight, sturdy branches of various lengths, and sharpen both ends. Securely stick the branches into the ground, side by side, and extending out from the base of the tree. Place bait (preferably meat) on the sharpened figure four stick.

Attach line and bait to the center section of the figure four and run it up and over a strong branch in the tree. Tie the free end of the line 1 foot from the up side end of a heavy, well-positioned log. The log should be 6 to 8 feet long and form a 25- to 30-degree angle between its high side and its low side, and the ground. When an animal tries to eat the meat, it will set off the trigger, and the upper end of the log will fall and drive its head and shoulders into the sharpened sticks.

Trip Line Mangle Snare
An animal caught in this snare will be mangled and killed. The trip line mangle snare is very similar to the fall log trap and is primarily used on

Trip line mangle snare.

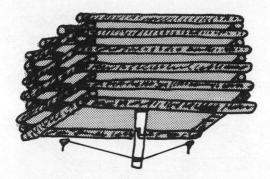

A box trap created using an L-shaped two-pin toggle trigger.

larger predatory game. Instead of using bait to trip the snare, however, this design uses a trip line that is run across an animal trail. To construct a trip line mangle snare, you will need two sturdy trees, one on each side of the animal trail. Set up a three-pin toggle (as outlined above) approximately 1½ to 2 feet high on one of the two trees. Attach the line to the lower crosspiece of the three-pin toggle, run it up and over a strong branch in the tree, and tie it 1 foot from the up side end of a heavy, well-positioned log. (Once again, the log will need to be positioned so that it strikes the animal when the trigger is released.) The log should be 6 to 8 feet long and form a 25- to 30-degree angle between its high side and its low side, and the ground. Tie another line to the trigger's crosspiece and attach it to a tree that is directly on the other side of the trail. The line's height should be about midleg to chest high on your intended game. When an animal walks on the trail it'll trip the line, and the upper end of the log will fall and mangle the animal.

Snares/Traps That Hold

Box Trap
A box trap is ideal for small game and birds. It keeps the animal alive, thus avoiding the problem of having the meat spoil before it's needed for consumption. To construct a box trap, assemble a box from wood and lines, using whatever means are available. Be sure it's big enough to hold the game you intend to catch. Create a two-pin toggle (see above) by carving L-shaped notches in the center of each stick. For the two-pin toggle to work with this trap, it's necessary to whittle both ends until they're flat. Be sure

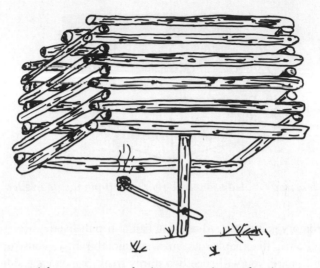

A box trap created using a one-pin toggle trigger.

the sticks you use are long enough to create the height necessary for the animal or bird to get into the box. Take time to make a trigger that fits well. Set the box at the intended snare site.

Secure two sticks at opposite ends, on the outside of one of the box's sides. Tie a line to each stick, bring the lines under the box, and secure them to the middle of the lower section of your two-pin toggle. Connect the two-pin toggle together, and use it to raise the side of the box that is opposite the two stakes. Adjust the lines until they're tight and approximately 1 inch above the ground. Bait the trap. When the animal or bird trips the line, it will be trapped in the snare. *Note:* A one-pin toggle trigger can easily be used in place of the design described here. (See illustration.)

Apache Foot Snare

The Apache foot snare is a trap that combines an improvised device (which can't easily be removed when penetrated) with a simple loop snare made from very strong line. This snare is most often used for deer or similar animals and is placed on one side of an obstacle, like a log. The ideal placement is directly over the depression formed from the animal's front feet as it jumps over the obstacle.

To improvise the device that the animal's foot goes through, gather two saplings (one 20 inches and the other 14 inches) and eight sturdy branches that are ½ inch around and 10 inches long. Lash each sapling together forming two separate circles and sharpen one end of the eight branches to a blunt point. Place the smaller circle inside the other and then evenly space the branches over both so that the points approach the center of the inner circle. Lash the sharpened sticks to both of the saplings.

When the animal's foot goes through the device, it will be unable to get it off. As it continues forward the strong simple loop snare will tighten down on its foot. When constructing a snare like this one, I often use a three-strand braid made from parachute cord, but any strong braid will work. The free end of the snare line should be secured to a large tree or other stable structure. Be sure to camouflage the snare's loop by covering it with leaves or a similar material. Any large animal caught in this snare should be approached with caution.

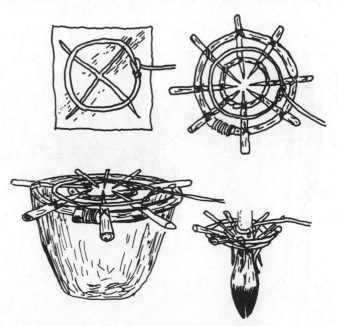

Apache foot snare.

Ojibwa Bird Snare

The Ojibwa bird snare is an effective snaring device, yet it requires time and materials to create. If you have both, it may be worthwhile to set one out.

Find a sapling that is 1 to 2 inches in diameter and cut the top off so it's approximately 4 to 5 feet high. To prevent birds from landing on the top, carve it into a point. The bait can also be attached here. Make a hole slightly larger than ½ inch in diameter near the top of the sapling. The perch will eventually be placed into this hole. Cut a stick 6 to 8 inches long and about ½ inch in diameter. If you prefer, you can sharpen one end of the stick and attach the bait there.

Using a piece of 3- to 4-foot line, make a slip knot or noose at one end. The noose should be 6 to 8 inches in diameter. One to 2 inches beyond the noose, tie an overhand knot. This knot is instrumental in securing the perch to the sapling until a bird lands on it. Pull the free end of the snare line through the hole in the sapling until the knot reaches the opening. Insert the perch into the hole, and use the knot to lightly secure it in place. If using the perch to hold the bait, be sure to bait it first. Tie a rock or heavy

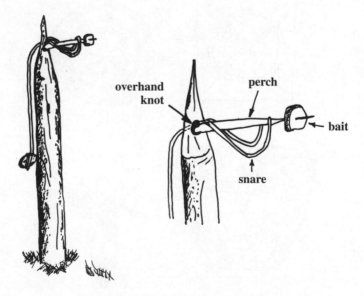

An Ojibwa bird snare using a rock.

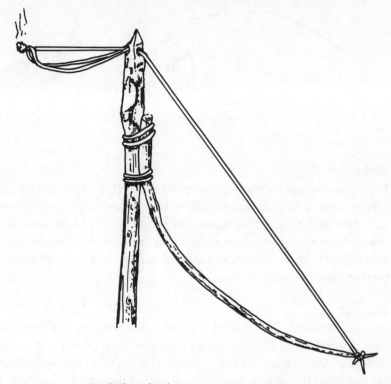

An Ojibwa bird snare using a sapling.

stick to the free end of the line. It must be heavy enough to pull the noose tight once the bird dislodges the perch from the sapling. Lay the noose on top of the perch. It may be easier to tie the rock to the line before inserting the perch into the hole. An alternative to the rock would be to cut a 3-foot-long sapling that is then attached to the back of the Ojibwa's pole (the top end should be below the perch's hole). Carve a small notch on the down side of the sapling so that the free end of the snare line can be attached. Finally, bend the sapling up and adjust the line's length so that when set, it will maintain the bend. The tension created by the bend in the sapling will cause the snare line to quickly tighten around the bird's foot when it dislodges the perch.

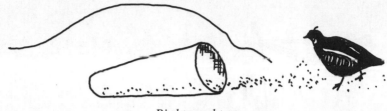

Bird tunnel trap.

Bird Tunnel Trap

Dig a funnel-shaped tunnel that narrows at its end. Using bait (bird seed, berries) create a trail that leads to the back of the tunnel. The bird will enter the tunnel while eating the seed and, once done, will be unable to back out since its feathers will become wedged into the tunnel's walls. This trap is most effective for birds that have guard feathers on their heads. (A quail is a good example of this.)

Bird Hole Trap

In a piece of wood, cut a small circle that is barely big enough for a bird's head to get through. Like the tunnel trap, this design works best on birds with guard feathers. Securely place the wood over a small hole and use seed, fruit, or other bird bait to lead the fowl toward the trap. Be sure to place some on the board and at the bottom of the hole. When the bird puts its head through the wood, its feathers will become wedged when it tries to withdraw its head. *Note:* This can be used with a jar, but its slick sides make it less effective.

Bird hole trap.

9

Stones and Bones

Today backcountry travelers have $200 knives made from the finest steel with the strongest handles—how would this knife be replaced if lost?

I watched in denial as the instructor took my knife. My knife, the tool I had become so reliant on. How would I prepare my fire? How would I build the triggers for my snares? How would I meet my needs? As he left me alone with only the clothes on my back and a small amount of parachute line, I wondered—what can I do to replace the most important tool I own? I needed to learn more about stones and bones.

STONES

Hammers, axes, clubs, mortars, pestles, and arrowheads are just a few examples of how stones have been used throughout time. Through the processes of flint knapping, pecking, and crumbling, most rocks can be transformed into these tools.

FLINT KNAPPING

Flint knapping is the art of making flaked stone tools. Percussion flaking is the process of creating a flake (blank) by striking one stone with another. The resultant blank can then be made into a knife or arrow point by using a pressure-flaking technique.

Flint Knapping Materials
 • Safety materials. The act of flint knapping is not without potential risk and you should always wear leather gloves, eye protection, long pants, leather to cover your legs, and shoes. In addition, working in a well-ventilated area is highly advisable.

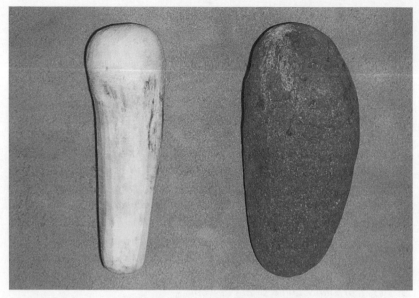

Hard hammer and an antler billet.

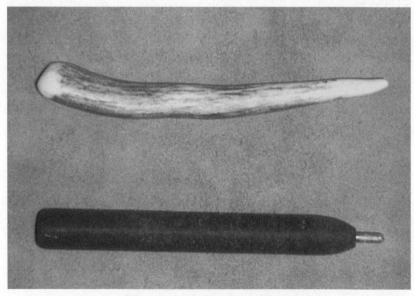

Antler tine and copper wire flakers.

- Hammer stones. A hammer stone is used to strike the stone. Stream-rounded cobbles are ideal for hard hammer flaking and antler billets are best when using a soft hammer technique. The size of the stone or antler billet will depend on the detail of work you are doing.
- Pressure flaker. A pressure flaker is used to create spear tips and similar items. Unlike the hammer that strikes your stone, this tool applies its force by pressing the flaker against the stone. The tine of a deer antler is the most commonly used pressure flaker. Nails, bone, and thick copper wire with improvised handles are other options.
- Stones. The most common stones used are obsidian (the easiest to use and recommended for beginners), basalt, rhyolite, chert, and flint. Man-made options can be found in glass and porcelain. The ideal material will be homogeneous, brittle, and elastic. Homogeneous stones are the same consistency throughout, lacking flaws and irregularities. There is a fine balance between rocks that are brittle yet elastic. A rock that is brittle and yet elastic will break easily but if not deformed to its breaking point it will return to its original shape. To understand flint knapping better I'd like to review a stone's nomenclature.
  — Core. A core is the piece from which the flakes are removed. It may be used to provide sharp flakes or be turned into a tool itself.
  — Flake. A flake is the material removed from the core. The flake is often used to make tools such as arrow points and knife blades.
  — Striking platform. The surface (usually flat) on both the core and the flake where the separating force is applied.

platform   **flake**

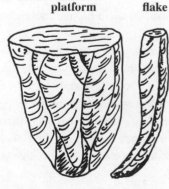

Platform and flake.

Percussion Flaking

There are four basic methods of percussion flaking:

- Hammer and anvil. In this technique, the core's edge is struck against an anvil (large stationary rock) to remove the flake. The biggest problems associated with this method are the lack of control and dangers related to flying flakes.
- Bipolar. Similar to the hammer and anvil except with this technique the core is placed on the anvil and struck with a large heavy hammer. This method is most often used on stones that are very difficult to work with. It has the same disadvantages as seen with the hammer and anvil.
- Hard hammer percussion. In this technique, the core is held in one hand and struck with the hammer stone. This method allows you to have more control over where the core is struck and how large the flake will be.
- Soft hammer percussion. In this technique, a hammer that is softer than the core is used. Common examples of this are soft limestone, deer antler, and bones. A blow to the core with a soft hammer starts a flake fracture, which it can then tear away from the core.

For our purposes I am going to discuss hard hammer percussion flaking. This method allows you to create both core and flake tools from a rock. Holding the stone in your less dominate hand while striking it with a hammer is a very simple way of visualizing this process. To prevent cuts, be sure to wear leather gloves and to place a leather drape over your lap. In addition, eye protection is advised.

To make tools from the core or resultant flakes, the rock must have a proper platform for you to strike. This platform must provide an angle with fewer than 90 degrees between it and the side of the rock. If the rock does not naturally have this angle, it will be necessary to create it by breaking the stone in half. I normally use a bipolar method to accomplish this.

Once you have a good platform, sit down and hold the stone—platform side up—in your hand and support the wrist on your leg (be sure to wear gloves, goggles, and use a lap mat). Approximately ¼ to ⅛ inch from the edge of the stone, strike the platform with your hammer using a downward angle of fewer than 90 degrees. The distance between the edge of your stone and where you strike determines the size of the flake. Too close to the edge and you only get chips; too far away from the edge and you proba-

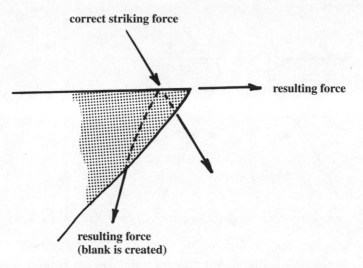

Strike the core at an angle of fewer than 90 degrees.

bly won't even produce a blank. You don't need to hit the core hard. In fact, in most cases you only need to guide the hammer stone down onto the platform.

On occasion you may have irregularities in your platform or its angle may be more than 90 degrees. Striking the stone from the opposite direction usually corrects this problem. This process is often referred to as faceting.

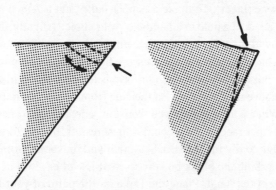

To increase a platform's angle, strike it from the opposite direction first.

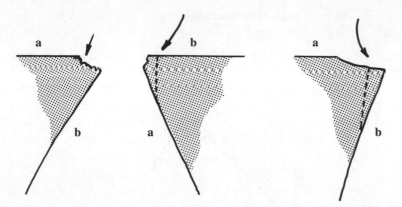

To remove platform irregularities, strike it from the opposite direction first.

Depending on your needs, the core and flakes can be used as is or can provide an excellent source from which to improvise. Pressure flaking is the next step.

Pressure Flaking

Pressure flaking is similar to percussion except on a smaller scale and the chips are removed by pressure instead of striking. Holding the flake in one hand and pushing chips off its beveled sides until sharp is a simple way of looking at pressure flaking. To do this you will need your safety gear, an abrader (usually a fine-grained sandstone), and a pressure flaker (antler tine or copper wire flaker). To make a copper flaker, cut a 2-inch piece of large diameter wire, drill a hole in a handle of your choice (slightly smaller diameter), and pound the wire into the hole until only ½ inch is showing.

As with hammer percussion, pressure flaking requires a proper platform. In pressure flaking, however, the platform is the edge itself. Ideally, the edge is slightly above the centerline on the side from which you intend to remove the flake. When a flake is removed from one side, the platform (edge) moves toward the other face of the piece. For best results, the platform needs to be sharp enough to dig into the pressure tool and prevent it from slipping off.

When working the blank be sure to wear a leather glove or use a leather pad to protect the hand. Place the flake on the palm of your hand (hold it between your fingertips and the heel of your hand) and support your hand by placing your wrist on your leg. Before starting, remove any thin sharp edges by rubbing your abrader over them toward the interior surface of the flake. This not only helps decrease the chances of cutting yourself but will also create a good platform from which to start. Use your flaker to remove as many flakes as you can before turning the blank over and doing the same on the other side (you should abrade the edge in the same direction as flaking before turning it over).

With pressure flaking the force is applied inward, slightly off the center plane, and in line with the surface of the flake you are removing. As you increase your force, apply a gentle downward motion until the flake breaks free. Too much downward force creates only short chips; too much inward force crushes the edge without removing any flakes. *Note:* If your edge is not bifacial, you will need to use a downward angle and force on the tip until enough short flakes are removed to create a bifacial point. In general, pressure flaking removes short chips from the rock. If you need to thin the blank, apply as much inward pressure as you can with just enough downward pressure to start the flake. If done right it will produce the long slender flakes needed to thin the piece. When notching the blank, continually

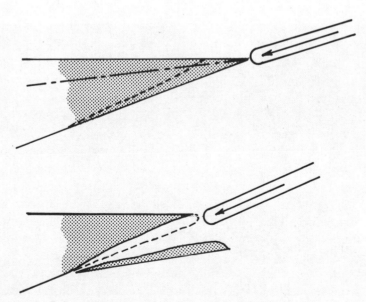

To remove a flake, use an inward and slightly off center force along with a gentle dowward motion.

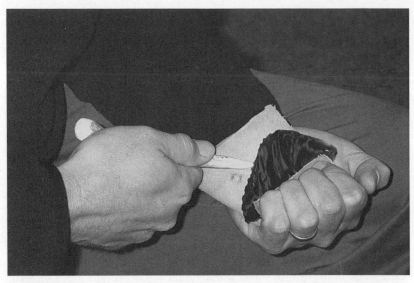

Ray Rickleman shows the proper technique for pressure flaking using an antler tine.

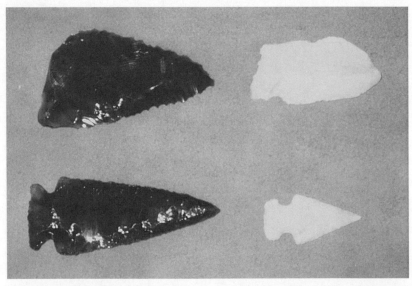

Various arrow and spear tips along with examples of the stone prior to pressure flaking.

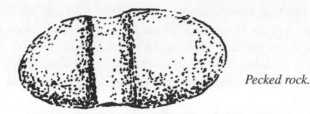

Pecked rock.

work the area with short controlled strokes, making sure not to compromise the flake's core causing it to break. A few examples of a final product are an arrowhead, knife blade, or spear tip.

PECKING AND CRUMBLING
Pecking and crumbling is the process of creating grooves and depressions in a rock. In most cases this is done to prepare a rock for a handle. Using a harder rock or hammer stone, repeatedly strike the rock you are working on, breaking down its grain until you create the desired result. Applying water to the stone while working on it will speed up the crumbling process.

BONE TOOLS
An animal provides us with many resources. Clothing and glue are just a few examples. Its bones can be used to make awls, needles, arrowheads, knives, scrapers, punches, spear points, clubs, and many other tools. Bones

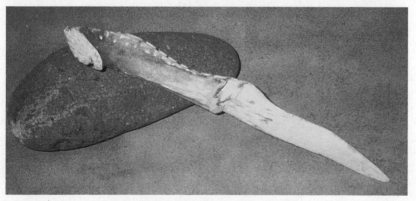

A knife made from an alligator's jaw.

are hard enough to accomplish many tasks and yet soft enough to easily transform into a workable item. To transform a bone into a tool, I first look at it and try to envision what need it can meet with the least amount of modification. Sometimes, I will just break it and work with the various sizes created. At other times, I score it—on each side—and use a hammer stone to break it in half. Either way, a sanding stone is used to develop the bone into the desired tool.

HAFTING

Hafting is the process of securing your stone or bone to a handle, which is often made out of wood. The two most common types are forked and wrapped (details on hafting arrowheads and spearheads are explained under the construction of each).

FORKED HAFTING

Cut a 2- to 3-foot branch of straight-grained hardwood (softwood will also work) that is approximately 1 to 2 inches in diameter. Six to 8 inches down

Hafting a forked branch to an ax.

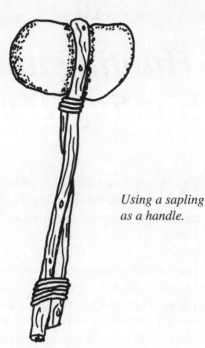

*Using a sapling
as a handle.*

from one end of the stick, snugly lash a line around the wood. I often use wet rawhide since it shrinks during the drying process creating a tight bond. With a knife, split the wood down the center and lash your stone between the wood and as close to the lashing as possible. Finally, secure the rock (bone or other material) to the stick with a tight lashing (done above, below, and across it). Using a strong forked branch is another method in which to create the same type of tool. Simply secure the rock between the two forked branches.

SAPLING HAFTING
This process is simple. Using a slender willow sapling (or similar material), wrap it twice around your pecked stone or bone and secure it in place with buckskin ties. The ties should be placed just below the wrap and at the bottom of the newly formed handle.

10

Hunting and Hunting Tools

At the local restaurants an 8-ounce steak costs between $8 and $24. The cow it came from was killed and butchered at the slaughterhouse. What would happen if the slaughterhouses no longer existed? How would we procure our meat?

> *As I lay under the tree, fully camouflaged and hiding, the approaching deer caught my eye. It moved to within three feet of my location before it stopped and stared directly at me. I didn't move and after a couple of minutes it resumed eating. Shortly after the deer was out of sight, a squirrel ran up onto my chest and ate its pine seeds. Since I was in training (hiding and trying to avoid being captured by aggressors), I made no movement on either occasion. This was my first encounter with camouflage and how it increased my ability to procure meat. I wanted to learn more.*

SPEAR

To make a straight spear, procure a long, straight sapling and sharpen one end to a barbed point. If practical, fire harden the tip to make it more durable by holding it a few inches above a hot bed of coals until it's brown.

To make a forked spear, procure a long, straight sapling and fire harden the tip. Snuggly lash a line around the stick 6 to 8 inches down from one end. Using a knife, split the wood down the center to the lash. To keep the two halves apart, lash a small wedge between them. (For best results secure the wedge as far down the shaft as possible.) Sharpen the two prongs into inward pointing barbs.

Flint-knapped tips can also be used to create a spear. To make one, attach a bone or rock tip to the front of your spear, using the techniques covered in the arrow-making section of this chapter.

A throwing spear should be between 5 and 6 feet long. To throw a spear, hold it in your right hand, and raise it above your shoulder so that the spear is parallel to the ground. Be sure to position your hand at the spear's center point of balance. (If left-handed, reverse these instructions.) Place your body so that your left foot is forward and your trunk is perpendicular to the target. In addition, point your left arm and hand toward the animal to help guide you when throwing the spear. Once positioned, thrust your right arm forward, releasing the spear at the moment that will best enable you to strike the animal in the chest or heart.

Using a spear to procure fish is a time-consuming challenge but under the right circumstances can yield a tasty supper. When using a spear you'll need to compensate for difference in light refraction above and below the water's surface. In order to obtain proper alignment, you'll need to place the spear tip into the water before aiming. Moving the spear tip slowly will allow the fish to get accustomed to it until you are ready. Once the fish has been speared, hold it down against the bottom of the stream until you can get your hand between it and the tip of the spear.

A forked spear made from a long sapling can also be used as a rodent skewer. To use it, thrust the pointed end into an animal hole until you feel the animal. Twist the stick so that it gets tightly snagged in the animal's fur. At this point, pull the animal out of the hole. Realize the rodent will try to bite and scratch you, so keep it at a distance. Use a club or rock to kill it.

Wooden forked spear.

BOW AND ARROW

A bow is an excellent method of increasing a projectile's speed and distance. Bows and arrows have been used for centuries by all cultures and many designs have been perfected over this time. Most bow construction follows simple guidelines. In fact, the biggest differences between most are whether they have a backing or not. A general rule of thumb is, the shorter the bow the greater its need for backing. Backing helps prevent it from breaking and decreases string follow, which in turn increases arrow speed. Backing will be discussed in more detail later. For our purposes I am going to describe how to make a self-bow (which doesn't have backing) from woods other than osage and yew. These woods include hickory, elm, ash, oak, birch, and walnut. They allow you to make the bow's back from the wood directly under the cambium layer and are far more forgiving to the first time bowyer. Building a bow begins with understanding the wood and how it should be prepared.

BOW: WOOD SELECTION AND PREPARATION

Tree Nomenclature

The vascular cambium, which lies between the bark and wood, is the main part of the tree that stays alive year-round. Although a tree's leaves, flowers, fruits, nuts, and seeds are alive they normally follow a cyclic process. The tree's outer bark and virtually all of its inner wood is dead. As the

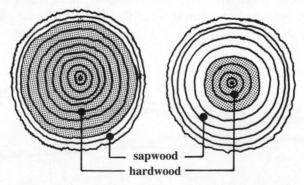

Sapwood is usually a lighter color than hardwood.

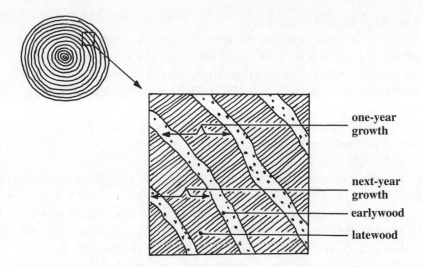

A latewood ring is normally darker and wider than an earlywood ring.

tree grows, its cambium creates new layers of dead inner wood and the most recently formed wood is called sapwood. Sapwood is relatively lighter (white to light tan) in color than the rest of the inner wood, called heartwood. As new layers are laid down by the cambium, each preceding layer moves inward converting into the darker heartwood. In most trees (osage orange is the exception) the sapwood is very strong and provides an excellent bow material.

In addition to the color changes created between sapwood and heartwood, annular rings can be seen. Two alternating rings, one dark and one light, usually represent a year of growth. The lighter ring is called earlywood, which is laid down as the tree comes out of hibernation. The dark ring represents latewood, which begins shortly after the tree rejuvenates and lasts until late fall when it goes back into hibernation. *Note:* Ash will have a dark earlywood and light latewood ring. Latewood is normally a wider ring that is far more dense and springy than earlywood is and as a general rule exposing earlywood on the back of a bow will compromise its strength. This is especially true with the harder woods. The ideal bow stave will have very thin earlywood rings and wide latewood rings.

Tree Selection and Preparation

It is best to collect your store (hickory, elm, ash, oak, birch, and walnut) during August when the bark is wet and sappy and a good solid layer of latewood has been laid down. (This differs from the normal process of collecting logs when the inner moisture is down—usually after the first thaw in mid-January). The ideal piece will meet the following criteria:

- 6- to 8-inch diameter.
- 2 inches longer than intended bow.
- Straight as possible.
- Free of knots and deformities (this is especially important at the far ends).
- Straight grained. A wood's grain runs from the center out like spokes of a tire or the cuts on a pie. To know if there is a twist in the tree grain, look at its bark. If it spirals up the trunk then the grain is twisted.

To decrease damage to the ends of your log, cut it with a saw and immediately seal the ends with varnish, paint, or Elmer's glue (at least 2 inches down the bark). Use a sledgehammer, wedges, and ax to split the wood into staves. If able, identify a grain and make your split along its natural path. Finally, strip it of its bark and cambium layer (which should come off easily). Remember, the wood directly below your cambium will be the back of your bow so be gentle when removing it. If you need to cut the wood in the winter, you can follow the same steps but it may be harder to remove the inner bark (cambium) without damaging the sapwood (back of the future bow). To compensate, I have heard of people placing the wood in a hot steamy shower for 20 minutes until the cambium becomes swollen and easier to remove. As a general rule a 4-inch log yields two staves, 6-inch provides three, 8-inch four, and a 10-inch log produces five staves. Be sure to always split from the bark side.

There is much debate on how to properly dry the stave. Some advocate letting it air dry for a year or more while others use the highly debated kiln to speed up the process. I am too impatient to wait years for a stave and too scared to use a wood that is kiln dried. I normally place my wood inside for 2 weeks and then move it to an area that can provide a constant temperature between 90 and 120 degrees until it's ready. In the summer, an attic or car work quite well as a hot box and can dry the wood in 1 to 3 months. The stave is considered ready when its moisture content is between 7 percent and

12 percent. Unless you have a moisture meter (a great tool to have), how will you know when this moisture content has been accomplished? Try weighing the wood every day and when it stops losing weight it has stopped losing moisture. As a general rule of thumb, wait another week and at this point the stave should have the proper moisture content and be ready to use.

BOW: MAKING A BOW

Cutting the Wood
The exact style of bow you build will be of personal preference. If you use a wood other than osage but still use the designs created for osage it is advisable to increase the bow's width by approximately 30 percent to achieve a similar result in power. A bow that is 66 inches long with 2-inch wide limbs that taper into its distal notches is an ideal design for hickory, elm, ash, oak, birch, and walnut.

Identify the back (sapwood side) and belly of your bow before doing anything. Always work on the belly side of the wood. Using a dull 12-inch drawknife, thin the wood down (on the belly side) until the stave is approximately 2 inches thick from back to belly. Be sure to follow the contour of the wood's back maintaining a constant thickness from end to end. If the back side dips in, so should the belly side. If you have a knot in the wood be sure to work around it—don't cut through it. Once the 2-inch width is reached, identify the stave's flattest path and mark a line down its belly from one end to the other. A chalk line works great for doing this. Decide where the bow's center will be on this line and mark it (this is commonly called the centerline). Make another mark 1 inch above and 3 inches below the centerline. This is where your handle will be. Next draw a line at the midpoint between the handles and the stave's ends.

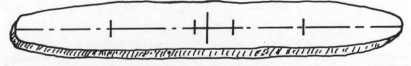

Marking the stave helps you develop its design.

Connecting the circles further defines the bow's shape.

Using a compass set at 1½ inches, make a circle inside the handle margins by placing its pencil on the outer handle line and its point on the centerline that runs from end to end on the stave. Make this circle on both the upper and lower handle lines. Next, draw a 2-inch circle at the midway point of the limbs (between the handle lines and the ends) using the line-line intersection as the reference point on where to place your compass's point. Finally, draw a ¾-inch circle at the far ends of the stave. Connecting the outsides of these circles provides the shape of the bow you will make.

Secure the board in a vise or similar item, with the edge of the wood facing up. If using a vise, be sure to pad the teeth so they won't damage the wood. With your drawknife, peel off the excess wood until just shy of your pencil markings. If doing this properly, the wood shaving should curl off the stave. Repeat on the other side. Using the outer edge of your handle circles draw a line from the back to the belly on each side of the wood. Using these four lines—two on each side—will provide a reference point for the handle while trimming is done on the belly side of the stave. Using your dull 12-inch drawknife, taper the bow's belly until the stave begins to resemble a bow (usually to around 1¼-inch thickness). To do this, start at the handle's reference points and draw the blade toward the end of each limb. What you do to one side should be done to the other. Be sure to follow the contour of the wood's back maintaining a constant thickness from end to end. If the back side dips in, so should the belly side. If you have a knot in the wood be sure to work around it—don't cut through it. Cutting through the knot will compromise the wood's strength. Besides, a knot can add some character to the bow.

The bow begins to take shape.

Floor Tillering

At this point you can begin floor tillering your stave. With the back of the bow facing you, place the lower end against something solid (perhaps your foot or the corner of a wall and floor), and hold the upper end firmly in your hand. With your free hand, pull the handle toward you while observing the flex of the bow's limbs. At first there may not be much of a flex but by the time you're done the limbs should bend evenly from handle to tip. If the bow doesn't bend, place it back in the vise—belly side up—and use the flat side of a sharp 8- to 10-inch coarse rasp (the rasp should have one round and one sharp side) to thin the limbs. Do twelve strokes to each side and then try to floor tiller the stave again. Repeat this process until the stave bends when tillering. Be patient—don't get in a hurry and take off too much. Once it begins to bend, look for flat spots and use a pencil to mark the beginning and end of where they appear. Place the stave back into the vise and work the marked area. Watch the grain (on the belly side) as it can help you gauge your progress. It should be centered with its point directed toward the ends of each limb. (See illustration.) If it is off center, then the side they run to is too thick. Repeat the floor tillering process until you can easily and evenly bend the limbs and you feel you are getting close to the final product. At this point you're ready to begin using a tillering board, but first you'll need to nock the stave's ends so that a string can be attached.

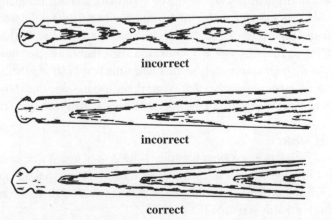

incorrect

incorrect

correct

Use the grain's feathering appearance to help you gauge your progress.

Self nocks.

To determine where the stave's nocks should be located, divide the bow's total length in half, measure this distance from the bow's exact center down both sides, and mark the final location with a pencil. Using a $5/32$-inch chain saw file (a pocketknife will also work), file out a string groove on each end of the wood. Begin by placing the file on your mark and perpendicular to the bow's side. Work the file at this angle until you begin to feel the wood with your finger. Be careful not to damage the back of the bow. At this point, begin filing on the belly side at a 45-degree angle that is directed toward the handle. Work both sides evenly so that when the bow is strung the line runs down the center of the bow's belly. When done, use a strong line (bowstring) that can be loosely attached to the nocks without actually stringing the bow.

Tillering Stick
A tillering stick is made from a strong 1- by 2-inch board that is approximately 4 to 5 feet long. It has a top groove for the bow's handle and multiple notches down one of its sides. The side notches allow you to increase the string's draw as you tiller the stave.

Set the bow's center on the top groove and pull the string downward, placing it in a notch that provides minimal pull on the bow's sides (usually 10 to 12 inches). Identify the stiffer limb and remove wood from its entire length (belly side) until both limbs look somewhat equal when drawn on the tillering stick. If a limb appears to have a hinge in it (an area that bends more then the rest of the limb) this will need to be fixed before moving on. Mark the hinge and remove wood on both sides of it until the entire limb bends evenly. Once the limbs pull evenly, string the bow so that there is a distance of approximately 3 to 4 inches between the belly side of the handle and the string (as the bow gets closer to the finished product this distance will most likely approach 5 to 6 inches).

Tillering with a Bow Scale
The next step in tillering is to view the limbs while weighing the bow's strength. The easiest way to do this is with a 2 by 2 and a bathroom scale. Cut a groove (slightly wider than the bow string) on top of the 2 by 2 and mark various draw lengths (from 10 to 30 inches) down its side. Attach a small piece of plywood to the bottom of the 2 by 2 and glue sandpaper to its underside (this will prevent slippage). Place the center of the bowstring into the wood's groove and the bottom of the board on the scale (be sure to zero out the scale first). Pull down on the handle to about the 15-inch mark

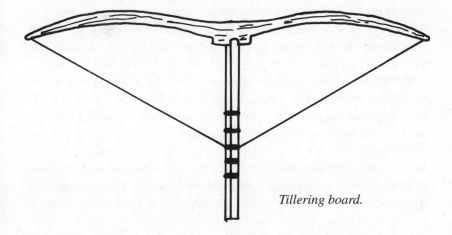

Tillering board.

and evaluate the bow's tiller. If unequal, remove wood from the stronger limb. Once the correct tiller is noted, then increase your pull in increments of 10 pounds (constantly adjusting the tiller with your rasp) until your final weight is reached (between 50 and 60 pounds for our bow's design). You will probably reach the desired weight with a very short pull. Don't forget to work the handle throughout the process so that a smooth transition occurs between it and each limb.

At this point exchange your coarse rasp for a fine cabinetmaker's rasp and use it to scrape a small amount off each limb until you reach full draw. Keep in mind that what you do to one side should be done to the other. The goal is to reach full draw while reducing the bow's mass but yet maintaining its draw weight. Don't get too overzealous and take off too much before checking the tiller. When you feel you're done, shoot the bow a dozen or so times and then check the tiller again. Do this for several days.

BOW: SINEW BACKING

As a general rule, the shorter the bow the greater its need for a backing (in most cases a 66-inch bow does not need a backing). Backing helps prevent it from breaking and decreases string follow, which in turn increases arrow speed. Sinew takes a majority of the stress off the back of the bow, which allows you to pull the string to your desired draw length.

Before applying the sinew, be sure to clean the bow's back of any grease or oils that it obtained from your hands, etc. If you have lye, mix it with water (1 part lye to 4 parts water) and brush it onto the bow taking great care not to get it on your skin or in your eyes. Once cleaned, rinse it thoroughly with warm water (or vinegar) and let it dry. To protect yourself from the lye, wear gloves, goggles, and an apron.

Gather several bundles of sinew (various lengths), a crock-pot or double boiler filled with hide glue (discussed in chapter 13) and heated to 115 to 120 degrees, smoothing tool (bone, dowel, or other such item), and an insulated cup full of warm water to place the smoothing tool in between each use. Dip a long bundle of sinew in the glue, allowing it to become fully saturated. While removing it from the glue, draw the sinew between your thumb and palm letting the excess glue fall back into the container. Place the center of this strip at the center of the bow's back and press it in place from center to

Place down the sinew in a staggered pattern.

end. Use the smoothing stick to help flatten the sinew onto the wood. Continue laying the bundles of sinew down until there is one continuous strip down the bow's center.

Using the center strip as a guide, place the rest of the sinew one limb at a time. The next strips (placed on each side of the center strip) will begin at the exact middle of the bow and each new strip will be placed in alternating starting points as seen on a brick wall. Once again be sure to use a smoothing stick. As the limbs narrow, excess sinew can run down the sides and onto the belly. In fact, this will add strength to the bow.

As a general rule, you want the sinew to be no more than 25 percent of the bow's width when it is dry. For most bows, you'll need to apply three to four total layers to the back. Many factors such as humidity, number of layers, and the amount of glue used contribute to the time it takes for the sinew to dry. It will take approximately 2 to 6 months for it to dry. Make sure it is completely dry before even thinking about drawing on it. Once dry the bow may require some minor retillering. A bow backed with sinew is not well suited for wet climates since too much moisture will cause the glue to dissolve and the sinew to fall away. To help protect it, you should consider finishing it like you would any other bow.

BOW: FINISHING THE BOW

Before applying any finish, sand away all tool marks. The bow can be finished with oils that penetrate the pores or by applying a protective covering such as varathane.

Some common oils used are tung oil, linseed oil, cedar oil, and animal fats (avoid using animal fats on sinew-backed bows). The oils work by penetrating the pores of the wood and multiple applications are required to create a decent waterproof finish. In order to maintain the finish, additional treatments are required at least twice a year and even more often when used in wet conditions.

When using a protective covering like varathane, as many as five coats may need to be applied to achieve adequate protection. Once done, use a very fine grade sandpaper to remove all the shine created by the finish. Although varathane is a good product, you will still need to coat the bow with a layer of paste wax at least once a year and more often when used in wet conditions.

BOW: BOWSTRING

Bowstring can be made from such sources as sinew, artificial sinew, rawhide, nylon, and cambium. You may fantasize about using a bowstring made from sinew but realize it is not always the best choice. In areas of high humidity or moisture, sinew will stretch and may even break. Therefore in such climates you may be better off choosing another material. No matter what you choose, make a two-strand braid from the material (covered in chapter 12).

Rick Sexton shows his self-bow.

To attach the bowstring, tie it to one of the bow's nocks and place that end down against the outside of your foot. Run the opposite knee slightly inside and against the bow's belly and let the handle rest against the leg. To tie the free end of the line to the upper nock, grab the high end of the bow and pull it down while pressing your knee outward on the belly. When done, the distance between the bow and string should be approximately the same distance as your fist plus the outstretched thumb.

ARROW
A bow is only as good as the arrow it shoots.

ARROW: SHAFT SELECTION
The exact type of material used to construct an arrow often depends on what is available in the area. Bowyers have used everything from split timber or saplings to small shoots to create a shaft that is strong, lightweight, and straight. Here are just a few examples of different materials that can be used to make arrows (you are not limited by this list):

river reed	river cane	cattail	bamboo
sitka spruce	douglas fir	Norway pine	Port Orford cedar
birch	dogwood	willow	serviceberry
osage orange	hickory	maple	black locust
oak	ramon	ash	hazel

ARROW: HOW TO MAKE AN ARROW SHAFT
The exact length of your arrow depends upon your draw (usually 25 to 30 inches). It is best to procure arrow blanks that are 4 to 6 inches longer than your draw length.

Arrow Shafts Made from Shoots
River reed, river cane, cattail, and bamboo can all provide an excellent and lightweight shaft for arrow making. Since they have a hollow or pithy center, however, you'll need to make a hardwood foreshaft that is inserted and secured to the front end. To decrease the amount of work you'll have to do, try to select shafts that are straight with a ⅜-inch diameter at the base. Make the lower cut ½ inch below a joint and the upper cut 3 to 4 inches beyond one. Cutting the lower end close to the joint provides stability and strength for the nock; cutting the upper end 3 to 4 inches beyond a joint provides an area for the foreshaft to be inserted. If green when cut, create a bundle of around a dozen or so and let them season in a cool dry place for several months. The exact length of your shaft will depend upon your draw (usually 25 to 30 inches).

When the shafts are ready, they will need to be straightened. To do this, heat them over a bed of hot coals until warm and then lightly bend and hold them into position until cool. To prevent the shaft from breaking it is best to bend it only at its joints. An arrow wrench (usually an antler with a hole drilled in it) will make this task even easier. Simply insert the heated shaft through the hole and use the antler to pry it straight. As with hand straightening, be sure to bend at the joints.

Arrow Shafts Made from Saplings
The perfect sapling will have a straight grain, be 3 to 4 feet long, and have a base about ½ inch in diameter. If you can, cut saplings in the winter when the sap is down, tie them together in bundles of twelve, and let them season for 2 to 3 months in a cool dry room. After several weeks, go ahead and scrape off the bark using a 90-degree angle between your knife blade and the wood. Once seasoned, use a coarse rock, grooved sanding block, or sandpaper to smooth the shaft down to a diameter of ¼ to ⅜ inches. The lighter the wood, the bigger the diameter should be. Your goal is to create something similar to a dowel you might find at the hardware store. At this point, prepare the shaft for straightening by heating it over hot coals and using the same techniques as discussed under arrows made from shoots.

Arrow Shafts Made from Split Timber
Sitka spruce, Douglas fir, cedar, and hickory are just a few examples of the many woods that can be used to make a split-timber arrow. Collect your wood using the same technique as you did when making a bow (there is no need to seal the ends). Try to select wood that has a good straight grain and is free of knots. Split the material into 1- to 2-inch wide shakes and store them in a warm, dry room for 1 to 2 months. For best results store them on top of each other using an alternating pattern (each successive row angled 90 degrees to the previous one) with scrap wood spacers between each row. This will allow air to circulate around the wood. In addition, turn the shafts over once a week to aid in the drying process. Once dry, use your knife to split the wood into 1-inch square sections. Next, with a hand plane create a square dowel that is about ⅜ of an inch. The exact size will depend on the wood you are using. The lighter the wood, the bigger the shaft's diameter needs to be. To do this, you'll first need to create a flat surface on one side.

Once done, place the flat side down and do the same on the other side so that the distance between the two is ⅜ of an inch. Repeat this process on the other two remaining sides. The final product should be a perfectly squared ⅜-inch dowel.

To transform the square dowel into a round one, plane off the four corners, which will create eight. Next, plane down the newly created eight corners, which creates sixteen corners and a nearly round shaft. Sanding is the last step. When done your goal is to have a perfectly straight and round dowel that is ¼ to ⅜ inch around.

ARROW: FINISHING THE ARROW

Nock the Arrow

The easiest way to nock an arrow is to tape two to three hacksaw blades together and saw a ½-inch-deep slot into the exact center of the shaft's end. For optimal arrow strength, make the cut at a 90-degree angle to the wood's grain. Use a rat-tail file to enlarge the nock until your bowstring almost fits (but still doesn't) and then finish with sandpaper. When done the string should snap into the nock with the application of only a slight amount of pressure. Wrap sinew around the arrow from the bottom of the nock to about 1 inch up the shaft. Glue is optional. If you don't have hacksaw blades, use your knife (man-made or improvised) to create the nock.

Cut and Seal the Shaft

You need to cut your arrow shaft to the appropriate length, which is a personal preference and usually ranges between 25 and 30 inches. Don't forget to adjust for the type of arrowhead you intend to use. To seal the arrow shaft, apply paint, lacquer, or oil. Regardless of what you use, avoid products that create an unnatural, shiny finish.

Attach an Arrowhead

If hunting small game, simply sharpen and fire harden the tip of your arrow shaft (this should be done before the shaft is sealed). If hunting big game, you'll need to attach an arrowhead to the arrow's shaft. Once again use the hacksaw blades to cut into the end of the shaft (where you'll be attaching the arrowhead) and create a perfectly centered split that is in line (parallel)

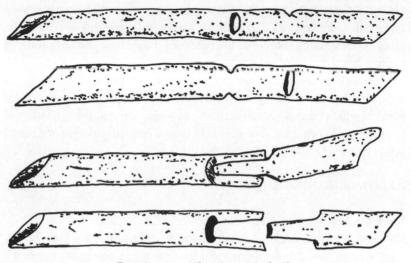

Creating a notch using your knife.

with the arrow's nock. Work both sides of the split until its width and depth allow a snug fit for your arrowhead. If you don't have hacksaw blades, use your knife to create a split that extends 1 inch down the middle of the shaft's end. Next, use your knife to work both sides until the depth and width provide a snug fit for your arrowhead.

Another method of using your knife to do this is to cut a small notch on each side of the shaft at the point where it should end. These cuts should be perpendicular to the nock at the other end. About ¼ inch above (toward

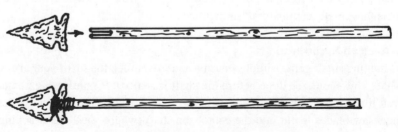

How to attach an arrowhead to a shaft.

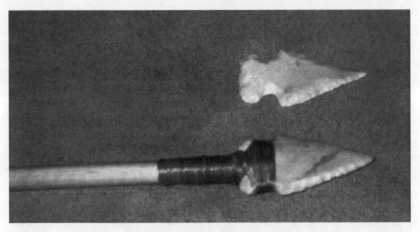

Arrowhead attached to a shaft.

the close end of the shaft) cut another notch on each side of the shaft (perpendicular to the first two). Finally, use a gentle up and down pressure on the excess shaft until it breaks free, leaving a deep notch. Regardless of how the notch is prepared, insert the arrowhead and secure it in place with hide glue and sinew.

For a shoot (a lightweight and somewhat fragile material), it is advisable to use a hardwood foreshaft that is inserted into its forward end. The 3- to 4-inch-long plug should be carved on one end and have a flint-knapped spear tip hafted to the other (as just described). To create a snug fit, bevel the shaft so that when it is fully inserted it slightly cracks the end of the shoot. To help hold the foreshaft in place, use hide glue and tightly wrap sinew around the end.

Fletching the Arrow
Fletching stabilizes the arrow's flight. Gather three feathers from the same side of a bird's wing or tail. Using a knife, cut down the center of the quill and split each of the feathers in half. *Note:* To make the splitting process easier, you may want to gently pound on the quills first. Separate the halved quills so that those from similar sides of the feather are used on the same arrow. Cut the feathers to preferred length (usually 3 to 6 inches) and trim ½ inch up on both ends of each feather's quill. This area will be used to tie

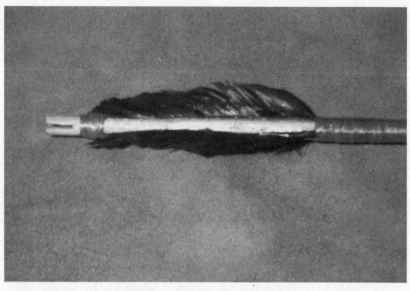

Fletching stabilizes the arrow's flight.

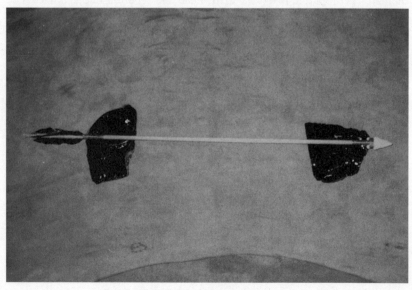

This arrow is ready to use.

the feather to the arrow's shaft. Next, trim the feather so that it has an even height from one end to the other (usually about ⅜ of an inch). Finally, smooth the inside of the quill so that it will conform to the arrow's natural curve when it is attached.

Apply hide glue to the quill side of the feathers and secure them, 120 degrees apart, with sinew. The hide-glue-soaked sinew should be tied at the top and bottom of the feathers. Place the feathers on the arrow (nock end) so the side that was attached to the bird is closest to the arrowhead side of the shaft. Let dry.

ATLATL AND DART

The word atlatl is derived from the Aztecs who used this throwing device when fighting the Spanish. A spear thrower, it is believed to be the predecessor of the bow and arrow. The atlatl, simply put, is a stick that is used to throw a light spear or dart. The stick increases the arm's extension, which in turn greatly increases the distance and velocity of the spear being thrown.

MAKING AN ATLATL

Most atlatls are 15 to 24 inches long, approximately 2 inches wide, and ½ inch thick. The handgrip is usually the heaviest end and most designs taper back toward a prong that fits into the notch located at the back end of the dart. Many different woods have been used to construct an atlatl. The lighter woods, however, will allow a better and faster throw. Juniper, cedar, and yew are three good options. To aid in throwing the dart, two loops are tied to the handle so that the thumb and index finger can slide through them when holding the atlatl. This allows you to throw the dart using a motion that is similar to throwing a baseball. Another option is to place the index and middle fingers through the loops and to adjust your throw appropriately. Some atlatl designs have a weight attached to their underside. These weights work as a counterbalance to the dart and they allow a hunter to hold the dart in a ready position for long periods of time. The exact position and weight of the counterbalance will depend on your atlatl design and the size and length of your spear. You will probably need to adjust it until it feels balanced when holding the atlatl and dart in the ready position. To protect the atlatl from the elements, I'd advise finishing it in a fashion similar to the bow (using either an oil or protective covering).

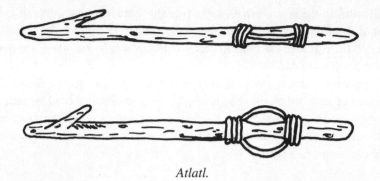

Atlatl.

ATLATL DART

Although I have heard of people using atlatl darts that are only 18 inches long, most are 4 to 7 feet long. The ideal material for the shaft is reeds, canes, or shoots. If you are lucky enough to find a straight sapling (or branch), however, it will also work well. Cattail, which can be found around the world in wet marshy areas, provides an excellent lightweight shaft for your dart. Attaching an arrowhead to the atlatl dart is done in the same fashion as described for making an arrow. The back of the dart needs a small grove (hole) that allows it to sit into the atlatl's notch.

HUNTING

Snares are excellent tools since they work for you while you attend to other things. At times, however, it may be necessary for you to actually hunt down your game. If this should be the case, take the time to prepare before going out. Wear dark clothes, camouflage your skin with dirt or charcoal, cover your scent with smoke or pungent plants from the local area, and try to stay downwind from the animal. In addition, try to hunt at dawn or dusk, as this is the most active time for many animals. Any of the following techniques can be used to hunt wild game.

TRACKING AND STALKING GAME

Tracking an Animal

To stalk an animal, you must first see it. If there is none in sight, you'll need to find it using the tracks and sign it leaves behind. You don't need to be an expert tracker to do this. You simply need a few basic skills that will allow you to determine where the best hunting and trapping area might be.

Animal Tracks and Pattern of Movement

An animal's track is simply the impression its foot leaves on the ground. As time passes, this impression is changed by the sun, rain, and wind along with insect and other animal overlay. All tracks begin to deteriorate soon after they are made. In addition, the type of ground in which the track is made will directly impact its longevity. As a general guideline, use the following to help you determine the approximate age of an animal's track.

• Crispness. Once an impression is made the effects of the sun and wind will begin to deteriorate its borders. The crisper its defined borders are, the fresher it is.

• Weather. If there has been a recent rain or snowfall, you can determine if the track occurred before or after it happened. The same can be said for dew and frost. If there is crisp dew on the ground but the track is absent of it, this is a good indication that the track is fresh.

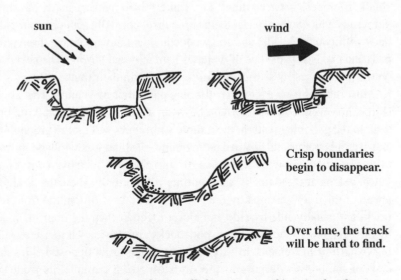

Over time, the wind and sun will destroy a track's crisp border.

• Evaporation. If you are in an area where the ground is dry but an imprint creates moisture, you can estimate how old the impression is based on the amount of moisture it still contains.

• Vegetation. If a track has new undisturbed growth within it, then it is old. If an animal's track contains compressed and broken young vegetation, it is usually a good indication of recent passage.

• Dislodged materials. Snow, dirt, sand, water, and so on will normally be sprayed forward in the direction of travel. As time passes, the displaced material will dry and harden and bond with its underlying surface, or it will evaporate.

For the purposes of this book, I am going to focus on three types of animal's tracks. These include rodents, rabbit and hares, and hoofed mammals. All three can provide an abundance of food for someone who is living in the wild.

Rodent Family

The white-footed mouse, gray squirrel, and woodchuck are all part of the rodent family. They all have a front foot with four toes with nails, three palm pads, two heel pads, and a vestigial thumb near the inner heel pad. Although these rodents have bigger hind feet, with five toes and nails, there are a few small differences between them. The white-footed mouse usually has three palm pads with two heel pads; the gray squirrel normally supports four palm pads with two heel pads; and the woodchuck is known to have three palm pads and two heel pads (one of which is hard to notice). *Note:* The heel pads on the hind feet of these rodents are rarely seen in their tracks.

Most rodents have a similar galloping pattern of movement. The woodchuck, however, tends to alternate between a galloping and a walking pattern. In the galloping pattern, the animal's front feet will hit the ground first and—as it continues its forward momentum—its hind legs will land in front of this position, allowing it to push off and continue its movement. Thus, when looking at these tracks, the imprints will normally show the hind feet ahead of the tracks created by the two front feet. In addition, the front feet tracks are usually side-by-side and closer together then the imprints made by the back feet. As mentioned, woodchucks are also known to use a walking pattern of movement. In this instance, limbs from opposite sides and ends of the body will move at the same time (for example, its front left

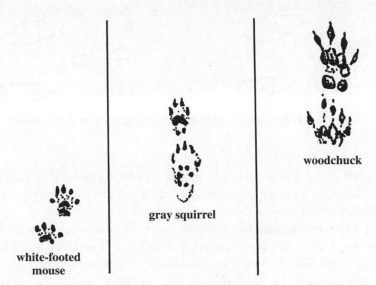

Tracks of various rodents.

and back right leg will move together) and as the animal moves, its hind track will usually land close to or partially on top of the front track.

Rabbit and Hare Family
The cottontail rabbit, snowshoe hare, and white-tailed jackrabbit are all part of the rabbit and hare family. They all have heavily furred feet with five toes and nails on the front and four toes with nails on the larger rear feet. The white-tailed jackrabbit is bigger then the cottontail and hare and thus, its tracks tend to be bigger and more deeply imprinted. (This doesn't account for the size variance seen with young or female jackrabbit.) However, the snowshoe hare can spread its toes out as much as 4 inches when traveling on snow. Thus, its tracks can be quite impressive in size but not necessarily

Most rodents use a galloping pattern when walking.

Rabbits and hares use a triangular galloping pattern of movement.

in depth. *Note:* The dense hair on a rabbit's or hare's foot makes it hard to see the animal's toe and toe pad marks (the toe pad marks are fairly small to begin with) when its tracks are made in snow.

Like rodents, rabbits use a galloping pattern of movement (covered under rodents). Unlike the rodent, however, its front feet will land with one in front of the other. When looking at these tracks, the imprints will normally show a triangular pattern created when the hind feet land ahead of the two front feet, which are one in front of the other.

Hoofed Mammals
The white-tailed deer, elk, and moose are all hoofed mammals. They all have feet that consist of two crescent-shaped halves and two dewclaws (located behind and just up from the hoof). They all leave heart-shaped

white-tailed deer

elk

moose

Tracks of various hoofed mammals.

Hoofed mammals use a walking pattern of movement.

prints with the sharp end pointing in the direction of the animal's travel. Adult male tracks made by moose, elk, and deer decrease in size in that order respectively. Elk tracks have a less drastic heart-shaped appearance, looking larger and wider then a deer's and smaller and rounder then a moose's.

Hoofed mammals use a walking pattern of movement similar to that described for a woodchuck (see preceding). With this type of movement, the animal's hind track will usually land close to or partially on top of the front track.

Understanding and Identifying an Animal's Sign

The term *sign* simply refers to any vegetation or landscape changes that indicate the animal has been there. This can include scat, food remains, bedding areas, trail corridors through the woods, stunted vegetation, and damage to trees and shrubs. When tracking an animal, learning to identify its sign is probably more important than finding a track. The sun, rain, and wind along with insect and other animal overlay will all affect the crispness of a track. The animal's sign, however, has a greater impact on the landscape and deteriorates at a far slower rate and thus may be the only indicator that an animal has been in the area. Here are a few basic ideas that may help.

• Scat (droppings). Every animal has droppings that are unique to it. Not only is scat useful in identifying that an animal is in the area, it can also help us determine how long ago it was there and what it has been eating. By taking the time to check the droppings for moisture, warmth, and content, you can provide yourself with a multitude of useful information.

• Food remains. Squirrels will often leave mounds of pinecone scales on stumps or fallen logs. The abundance and freshness of these mounds will help you determine if squirrels are active in the area. Hoofed mammals and rabbits browse on saplings and leaves. A deer will often leave a frayed top, whereas rabbits leave it looking like it was cut at a 45-degree angle with a knife. A good indicator of recent deer or rabbit activity would be a branch that has a fresh and white inner surface versus one that is brown and weathered

• Bedding areas. Rodents tend to live in underground dens or tree nests. If a nest is seen, watch for activity and look for other sign in the area. If an opening to an underground den is spotted, look for other sign in the area. Don't forget to evaluate the opening for spider webs or dead pine needles covering the entrance, as this usually indicates a lack of activity. Hoofed animals tend to disturb an area when they bed down. Bent-over grass, scraped dirt, and scraped snow are good indicators of a bedding area. If grassy, then look at how far it is displaced toward the ground. If it is well worn, it may be one that is frequently used; if fresh and appearing new, it may have been just a napping spot. If the snow has been scraped, does it look fresh or has there been a frost or new snowfall since the bed was created.

• Trail signs. Often an animal's trail can be easily identified, especially when looking for rabbits or hoofed animals. Animals, like humans, tend to take the path of least resistance whenever they can. After time, trails that lead from a bedding area to a water source can become very pronounced. A less traveled trail should be evaluated for recent activity by looking for vegetation displacement (vegetation that is bent, broken, flopped over, or pressed in), trees with displaced bark, pine needle movement, and recently broken twigs on the ground. *Note:* Broken twigs will usually lay in a V position with the point indicating the direction of the animal's travel and any other displaced vegetation will usually do the same.

Stalking an Animal
Once you have located your food source, if you intend to hunt it, you will need to use good stalking techniques. Staying downwind, move when the animal's head is down. I once heard that an animal (deer) will keep its head down for approximately 20 seconds while feeding and then lift it up to look around for movement. As a general rule, move for 10 seconds and then stop, staying perfectly still. Wait for the animal to pick up its head, look around and start grazing again, before moving for another 10 seconds. If the animal looks up while you are moving, freeze. As long as you don't move, it will

think you are a tree stump and will not comprehend that you're getting closer. If the creature is close to a creek, you may be able to move quicker without it hearing you. In addition, realize that noise is bound to happen. The key is to freeze (if you make noise) until you are sure the animal is comfortable. Getting close enough to use your weapon will take practice and skill.

DRIVING

Often done with a team of hunters, driving is a process of moving an animal into an awaiting ambush. Several members of the hunting party actually make themselves known to the animal and walk toward it, constantly adjusting to ensure that the animal follows a certain path. This method works best when the creature can be funneled into a valley or similar location.

CALLING

Understanding that animals communicate with each other is the first step in learning how to call them in. I have often kissed the back of my hand (making a short smacking sound) or scrapped two mussel shells together to attract a curious squirrel. Changing how I kiss my hand by making a long drawn out squalling sound can draw predators who think I am a hurt rabbit. This sound has also been known to catch the attention of a moose if it is done just right. Banging antlers together often attracts deer during their rutting season. Some hunters have perfected the art of attracting elk or duck by blowing on a blade of grass. Take the time to listen to the creatures in your area and practice different techniques of imitating their sounds. If perfected, you can draw the animal to your location—making the hunt a lot easier.

STAND (AMBUSH) HUNTING

Observe an animal's behavior, look for its sign, and select an ambush location that is downwind from the animal's approach.

11

Cooking and Preserving Meat

Gas and electric ranges allow us to cook our food. What would you cook on if they no longer existed?

> *After several days without food I was happy when it became available. The squirrel, rabbit, and goat always tasted great. I've eaten an animal's eyes, lungs, kidneys, heart, and even made sausage from its blood. Although I was often in a hurry to stuff my face, I'd take the time to cook my food. The warm meals not only nourished my body but they also fed my spirit.*

WHY COOK?

In addition to killing parasites and bacteria, cooking your food can make it more palatable. There are many different ways to prepare game and some are better than others from a nutritional standpoint. Boiling is best but only if you drink the broth, which contains many of the nutrients lost in the cooking process. Frying tastes great but is probably the worst way to cook since a lot of nutrients are lost during the process.

BOILING

Boiling is the best method, since all the vital nutrients of the food product can be gained by consuming the broth. If no container is available, it may be necessary to improvise one. You might use a rock with a bowl-shaped center (avoid rocks with high moisture content, as they may explode), green bamboo, or a thick, hollowed-out piece of wood that can be suspended over the fire.

If your container cannot be suspended over the fire, stone boiling is another option. Use a bed of hot coals to heat up numerous stones. Get them really hot. Set your container of food and water close to your bed of hot stones and add rocks to the container until the water begins to boil. To keep the water boiling, cover the top with bark or another improvised lid and keep it covered except when removing or adding stones. Don't expect a rolling rapid boil; however, a steady slow bubbling should occur.

BAKING

Baking is the next best method of preparing meat to eat. There are several methods I use to bake game.

MUD BAKING

I often use this method to cook fish and fowl. When mud baking there is no need to scale, skin, or pluck the fish or bird in advance since scales, skin, and feathers will come off the game when the dried mud is removed. Use mud that has a clay texture to it and tightly seal the fish or bird in it. The tighter the seal the better it will hold the juices in and prevent the meat from

Mud baking.

drying out. Once sealed, place the meal into a hot bed of coals so that it has an equal covering of coals both above and below it. A medium-sized bird or trout will usually cook in about 15 to 20 minutes depending on the temperature of your coals

LEAF BAKING

Wrapping your meat in a nonpoisonous green leaf and placing it on a bed of hot coals will protect, season, and cook the meat. When baking mussels and clams, seaweed is often used (when the shells gap open they're done). Avoid plants that have a bitter taste.

UNDERGROUND BAKING

Underground baking is a good method of cooking larger meals since the dirt will hold the oven's heat. Dig a hole slightly larger than the meal you intend to cook (it needs to be big enough for your food, the base of rocks, and the covering). Line the bottom and sides with rocks (avoid rocks with high moisture content, as they may explode) and start a fire over them. To heat rocks that will be used on top of your food, place enough green branches over the hole to support another layer of rocks. Be sure to leave a space to add fuel to the fire. Once the green branches burn through and a bed of hot coals is present, remove the fallen rocks. Place green twigs onto the coals followed by a layer of wetted green grass or nonpoisonous leaves. Add your meat and vegetables and cover them with more of the wet grass or leaves, a thin layer of soil, and the extra hot rocks. The hole is then covered with dirt. Small meals will cook in 1 to 2 hours; large meals in 5 to 6 hours.

FRYING

Place a flat rock on or next to the fire (avoid rocks with high moisture content, as they may explode). Let it get hot, and use it in the same fashion as you would a frying pan.

BROILING

Broiling is ideal for cooking small game over hot coals. Before cooking the animal, sear its flesh with the flames from the fire. This will help keep the juices, containing vital nutrients, inside the animal. Next, run a nonpoisonous skewer (a branch that is small, straight, and strong) along the underside of the animal's backbone. Finally, suspend the animal over the coals, using any means available.

METHODS OF STORING FOOD

KEEP IT ALIVE

If possible, keep all animals alive until ready to consume. This ensures that the meat stays fresh. A small rodent or rabbit may attract big game so be sure to protect it from becoming a coyote's meal instead of yours. This doesn't apply, of course, if you are using the rodent for bait.

WINTER STORAGE

In winter, freeze the meat into meal-sized portions to avoid unnecessary spoilage from constant thawing and freezing. Another winter option is to bury the food in a snow refrigerator.

SUMMER STORAGE

During nonwinter months you can create a refrigerator by digging a two-foot hole in a moist, shady location and wrapping your food in a waterproof container, before surrounding it with vegetation, and placing it inside the pit. Cover the food with sticks and dirt until the hole is filled.

METHODS OF PRESERVING MEAT

SUN DRYING

Use the long, thin strips of meat you cut when butchering the animal. Hang the meat in the sun out of animals' reach. To do this, run snare wire or line between two trees. If using snare wire, be sure to skewer the line through the top of each piece of meat before attaching it to the second tree. If using other line, hang it first and then drape the slices of meat over it. For best results, the meat should not touch itself or another piece.

SMOKING

Use the long, thin strips of meat you cut when butchering the animal. Construct a smoker and use it as follows:

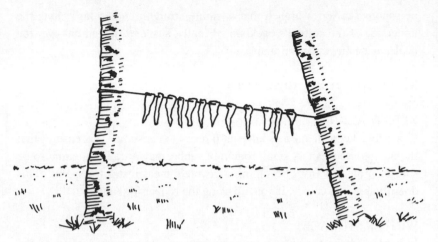

Sun drying meat is an effective method of preserving it for later consumption.

- Build a six-foot-tall tripod that is lashed together.
- Attach snare wire or line around the three poles, in a tiered fashion, so that the lowest point is at least 2 feet above the ground.
- If using snare wire, skewer the line through the top of each slice of meat before extending it around the inside of the next pole. If using other line, hang it first and then drape the strips of meat over it. For best results, the meat should not touch itself or another piece.
- Cover the outer aspect of the tripod with any available material, such as a poncho. Avoid contact between the outer covering and the meat. For proper ventilation, leave a small opening at the top of the tripod.
- Gather an armload of green deciduous wood, such as willow or aspen, and prepare it by either breaking the branches into smaller pieces or cutting the bigger pieces into chips.
- Build a fire next to the tripod, and once a good bed of coals develops, transfer the coals to the ground in the center of the smoker. Continue transferring coals as needed.
- To smoke the meat, place small pieces or chips of green wood on the hot coals. Once the green wood begins to heat up, it should start to smoke. Keep adding chips until the meat is dark and brittle—about 24 to 48 hours. At this point it is done.

• Since an actual fire will destroy the smoking process, monitor the wood to ensure it doesn't flame up. If it does, put it out, but try to avoid disrupting the bed of coals too much.

BLOOD SAUSAGE
After an animal has been killed, slit its neck and collect the blood in a container. Mix all of the scrap meat with the blood and cook it slowly over a

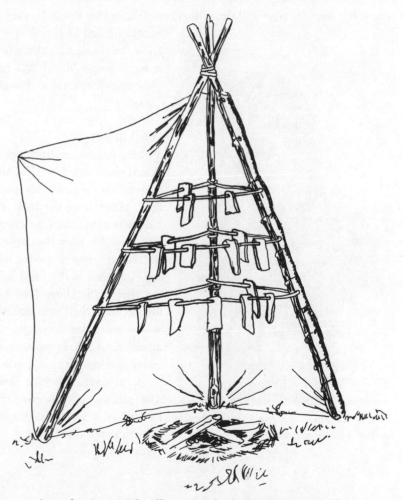

A smoker is a quick, efficient method of meat preservation.

warm fire. Once it has become similar to hamburger in consistency, it is ready for the next step. The intestines from medium to large game animals provide a perfect skin for your blood sausage. You will need, however, to clean them (inside and out) and wash them thoroughly in hot water before using. Cut the intestine into 6- to 8-inch sections and use line to tie off one end of each. Next, pack the cooked blood and meat into the skin so that it is tight—but not so tight as to tear it—and tie off the open end. Finally, smoke the sausage in the same fashion as described above for meat strips. The smoking time will depend on many factors but it usually ranges between 6 and 12 hours. You'll know the sausage is done when it is no longer moist and has the consistency of store-bought sausage.

Here is my daughter Jenna Davenport's idea of a well-rounded meal.

PEMMICAN

Making pemmican from dehydrated meat, dried berries, and suet tallow (animal fat most often taken from the loin and kidney area) creates an excellent meal for later use. Pound the berries into a paste, add dry, pounded jerky, and mix together with tallow. Roll the mixture into a ball and store in a sealed container out of animal and insect reach. In most cases, pemmican can be safely stored away for several months. *Note:* The process of rendering fat into tallow is covered in chapter 5 under lamps and stoves.

12

Containers and Cordage

What did we do before the invention of modern pots and pans, porcelain, and Tupperware?

After days without food, I had finally caught a rabbit. My stomach growled with anticipation while my mind flooded with thoughts of how I'd prepare it. I knew I needed to boil it in order to acquire all of its nutritional value, but how? When I was in the Scouts I had always taken a cooking kit and eating utensils to the woods. Now I had none. That night I cooked the rabbit directly over the fire while I made my first wooden bowl from the fire's coals. The next rabbit I caught was boiled.

CONTAINERS
Containers provide you with the ability to cook, store, and transport various liquids and solids. They can be created from animal stomachs or rawhide, wood, weaved baskets, or clay.

CONTAINERS CREATED FROM ANIMALS
Shaping, drying, and using an animal's stomach is the most common example of creating a container from large game. The easiest way to do this is to pour sand into the stomach, shape it, and let it dry. Once dry, simply pour out the sand. These containers hold their shape fairly well and tend to last a long time. In addition to the stomach, rawhide can be shaped using the same sand method. Other options include the animal's skull, hoofs, or pelvis.

CONTAINERS CREATED FROM WOOD
Find a log that when split in half provides the dimensions of the bowl you want to create. Split it in half lengthwise and place a hot red coal in the

Using a coal to make a wooden bowl.

center of the inner surface. Gently blow on the coal until it no longer glows or appears to have stopped burning into the wood. Dump it out, scrape away the char until good wood is exposed again, and place another coal onto the fresh surface. Repeat this process until done. Once you have the shape you want, scrape the bowl's inside surface until it is smooth, and work its outer surface until you achieve the desired shape.

CONTAINERS CREATED FROM BARK

Bark is a versatile resource that can be used to meet many of our needs. Maple, willow, birch, cedar, and juniper bark are often used to create a container. Birch bark is probably the easiest to use. It can be gathered from a live tree or one that has recently died. To procure the bark, cut a large rectangular piece (be sure to cut all the way through the bark), pry a corner free, and peel it from the tree. Do not ring the tree when doing this or you may kill it. If you don't intend to work the bark right away, soak it in water until you can get to it. This prevents it from drying out and becoming brittle. Lay the bark side down (side that was not against the inner tree) on a level surface, identify the center between the two ends, and using that as your guide, score (don't cut) two opposing oblique shapes that create an eye shape. (See illustration.) The score should allow the bark to bend but not break. Using the score as your guide, fold the ends together so that the eye-shaped area becomes the bottom of your soon-to-be container. As the sides are brought together the bottom should naturally create a slight upward curve. To make the sewing process easier, go ahead and mark the sides while they are together. The marks should be close to the edge but not so close as to split the bark. Lay the bark flat and drill the holes. To help stabilize the container's opening, it is advisable to wrap a sapling around it. In order to hold the sapling in place, you'll need to drill holes at the top of both ends. These holes need to run in an alternating diagonal sequence with one close to the top edge and one ½ inch below. (See illustration.) Once all the holes are drilled, fold the container together and sew the sides together with cordage or rawhide. Wrap the sapling around the top and hold it in place by lacing the cordage or buckskin around it (using the alternating holes). For ease of transport, attach a buckskin or cordage handle to the top.

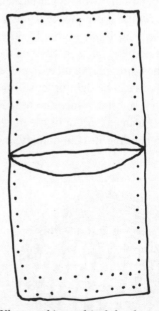

When making a birch bark container, score the bottom and make holes on the sides and top for your cordage.

BASKETRY

Baskets made from leaves, bark, and sticks provide unlimited uses. Willow, dogbane, cattail, grass, inner bark and outer bark, and vines are the most often used materials. Regardless of what you use, the material will work better if dry, not green. To make the dry material pliable before use, soak it for ½ hour or more in warm water. When making a basket the words "warp" and "weft" are used in describing the process:

• Warp: once done forming the basket's base, these are the vertical pieces. Warp material often comprises stiffer branches like willow.

• Weft: all the horizontal pieces that are threaded (at 90-degree angles) into the warps. Weft material often comprises more pliable material like cattail leaves.

There are three basic styles of basketry: weaving, twining, and coiling.

Basket Weave

Select your warp material trying to use pieces of similar diameter and lay four on top of four so that the centers are perpendicular (for bigger baskets use more then four). To create the base, intertwine these pieces using an over-under weave making sure to alternate how each one starts. In other words, if a warp starts by going under the first perpendicular piece, then the warp next to it would start by going over the same perpendicular piece. Depending on the basket's intended use, the base can be tight or loose simply by how close these warps are placed to one another. Once the base is done, bend the warps into a vertical position. If using a hard or brittle material, you may need to slightly score it before bending it. If in a hurry, the

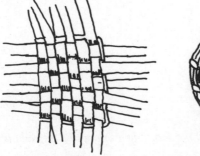

Making a basket using an over-under weave.

This basket's bottom was made by tying four warps on top of and perpendicular to another four warps and then using an over-under weft pattern.

Dawn-Marie North holding an improvised basket.

base can be started by simply tying the top four warps to the bottom four (perpendicular) and then using an over-under weave for the wefts.

Select wefts of similar diameter and begin using an over-under weave that circles around the warps. When splicing from one weft to another make sure they overlap at least two warps. When the wefts are within 2 inches of the warp tops, stop. Cut all the inner warps flush with the wefts and tuck the outer warps down inside the second or third weft from the top. Once again, you may need to score the warps to get a proper bend in them.

Twined Weaving

Twining is done in a similar fashion to the basket weave. Instead of weaving one weft around at a time, however, the weft is bent in half and weaved in a figure eight pattern. Creating the base and finishing the top can be done the same way as described in basket weaving.

Coiled Baskets

The coiled basket is a simple process of circling a coil (a small bundle of willow, cattail leaves, or similar material) on itself while connecting each new layer to the previous one. To start the coil, tie several pieces together and begin spiraling around the end. Continue out until you have formed

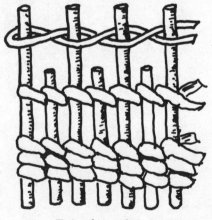

Twined weaving.

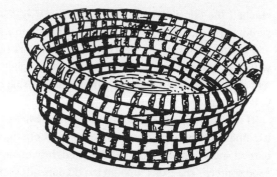

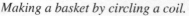

Making a basket by circling a coil.

the desired base size and then start going up. To hold it all together, use a strong pliable fiber (like you'd choose for cordage) and wrap it around one coil and through the next. The tighter you pull the two coils together the tighter the basket.

POTTERY

Pottery is an excellent method of creating containers that can be used for both storage and cooking. Although a process that needs to be learned through trial and error, once learned it is well worth the time spent.

Finding Clay

Clay is most often found along stream banks, ponds, and road cuts. It may be dry or wet. Either way, try to dig down or into your source to procure clay that is free of debris. Realize that all clay is not the same and in fact not all clays will work for making pottery. With this in mind, once you have found a source of clay you are ready to begin.

Preparing the Clay

If the clay is wet, simply free it of debris. If the clay is dry, rewet it. Begin by breaking it into as small particles, placing it into a container, and mixing it with water until a watery solution is obtained. After several minutes pour off the top water. Cover the container and let the clay sit for several days. During this time, pour off any new top water that forms. Once it has reached the consistency of molding clay it is ready to use. If you're not sure it is ready, roll out a foot-long section that is about ¼ inch in diameter and try to tie it into an overhand knot. If it is pliable enough to do this without breaking, use it. Getting the clay's consistency right is an important step. Clay that is too wet will not hold a shape and clay that is too dry will crack as you work it.

If the clay constantly slumps no matter what you do, you probably need a temper. A temper adds stability and will help the clay hold its form. Sand, burned shells, grass, or previously fired, broken, and crushed pottery are all good sources. The exact amount to add depends on variables from the size of the container to the type of clay you are using. Experiment with the clay you are using until enough temper has been added to allow it to hold its form while being worked.

Constructing a Small Clay Pot

Take a baseball-sized piece of clay and work it with your hands until it is round. Take time to work out all the air pockets, which may be inside the clay. Using your fingers or thumb, create a depression in the center and

Making a small clay pot.

begin pinching the sides (between your thumb and fingers), slowly enlarging the pot. Work around the container trying to create a constant thickness between the sides and the bottom (between ¼ and ½ of an inch). Once you have the desired initial shape, wet your pointer and middle fingers and slip them inside the pot—working them back and forth—smoothing the inner surface. Use your hand to smooth the outside surface. Be sure to maintain the container's thickness throughout this process. If an area is too thick, the pot will dry unevenly and probably break during the firing process. Set the bowl in an area that is free of sun and wind and let it dry. Once the opening has dried enough to support the weight of the container, be sure to turn it over so that the bottom will dry. Continue turning it several times a day until completely dry.

Constructing a Large Clay Pot

To create a larger container, start by making a small clay pot as just explained. Once it is formed, put wet leaves (or similar material) on the opening lip and set it aside for several hours. This will allow it to firm up somewhat while keeping the opening moist enough to add additional clay. Once the bowl appears to be solid enough to continue, remove the leaves and begin adding coils to the rim. Coils are rolled clay that is ¼ to ½ inch wide and long enough so that both ends touch when wrapped around the bowl's opening. Place the coil on the opening, then score them together with your fingernail or a bone (inside and out). Next, use your fingers to join the coil and bowl together until they appear as one. Continue to add coils until you achieve the desired size or you start to worry about the clay's ability to hold its weight. If the latter is the case, let the bowl dry while keeping the lip wet and when ready repeat the process. Once done, dry in the same manner as for a small pot.

Finishing

Once the container is completely dry and smooth, burnish the inside. To do this, put a small handful of sand inside the bowl and work it around with a piece of leather. Another method of burnishing the inside is to work it with a small round pebble or bone until smooth. If you desire a decorative outside, do it before drying is complete. Rolling cordage or corn over the surface will provide a nice appearance as will pressing wheat or making a decorative etching.

Jamie Davenport makes her pot bigger by adding a coil of clay to its top.

Firing the Pot

This is where most pottery containers are lost. Try to do this on a calm day without wind. Wind will create a constant fluctuation in the heat, which in turn will increase the likelihood of your pot's breaking. There are many different methods of firing a pot. Some people use charcoal barbecues, some use cow patties to hold a coal, while others make a natural kiln. Since charcoal and cow patties are not always available and making a natural kiln is not always practical, I am going to explain how to fire a pot using a simple wood fire.

Scrape an area big enough for your pots and line the bottom with rocks. Build a fire around it so that none of the flames touch the pottery and let it burn for about two hours. After the two hours have passed, slowly begin pushing the fire toward the pots and let it burn until the containers are glowing red. At this point, let the fire burn down and allow the containers to slowly cool before you begin using them.

CORDAGE

Improvised cordage (line)—from Mother Nature's resources—expands our ability to meet various daily needs. Fishing line, belts, and rope are just a few examples of the various items you can create. Cordage can be made from various materials such as plants, outer and inner tree bark, animal products (sinew, hide, and so on), and various man-made products (parachute line, twine, and so on). The best rope-making materials have four basic characteristics:

- Fibers need to be *long* enough for ease of work.
- Fibers need to be *strong* enough to pull on without breaking.
- Fibers need to be *pliable* enough to tie a knot in without breaking.
- Fibers need a *grip* that allows them to bite into one another when twisted together.

Regardless of what you use, as long as it meets these criteria it should work. Some examples of various options are listed below:

Example	Preparation
Stalks of fibrous plants	Examples include stinging nettle, milkweed, and dogbane. To prepare, pound dry stems, remove woody outer stalks, clean and use remaining fibers. Be careful when removing the outer wood that you don't break the inner fibers.
Cattail and rushes	Pound the leaves between rocks to start the breakdown process. Soak for several days, occasionally working the leaves with your hands. Remove the leaves from the water and if any of the outer cellulose is still present, scrape it off with a knife (use a 90-degree angle).
Yucca leaves	Prepare the same as cattail. Yucca can be used without soaking by simply scraping away the cellulose first.
Grasses and weeds	It is best to use grasses and weeds when they are green.

Example	Preparation
Trees	Willow, elm, spruce, cedar, and juniper are just a few examples. In most cases the inner bark is what you'd use. It's best when the tree is near dead since in this state much of the inner bark's moisture has dissipated.
Animal products	Hair, wool, sinew, rawhide, and buckskin can all be used. A lot of animal products, however, are not suited for wet conditions. Sinew, rawhide, and buckskin should be wet when used for lashing, but for cordage, make sure they are dry before beginning.

SPINNING A CORD

Using any material that meets the characteristic of good cordage, twist it between your thigh and palm. Add additional fibers to the free end as needed to make one continuous cord that can be used to create a two-strand, three-strand, or four-strand braid.

TWO-STRAND BRAID

The two-strand braid is an excellent all-around line that can be used for many improvising tasks. For tasks where a lot of weight will be applied to the line, however, a four-strand braid would be a better option. Use the following steps to make a two-strand braid:

• Using spun cord, grab it between the thumb and forefinger of your left hand so it measures two-thirds of its length on one side and one-third on the other.

• With the thumb and pointer finger of your right hand, grasp the fiber that is farthest away from you. Twist it clockwise until tight and then move it counterclockwise over the other strand. It is now the closer of the two.

• Twist the second strand (which is now the farthest away) clockwise until tight and then move it counterclockwise over the first strand.

• Continue this process until done.

• Splicing will need to be done as you go and this is the reason for the two-thirds and one third split. Splicing both lines at the same location would

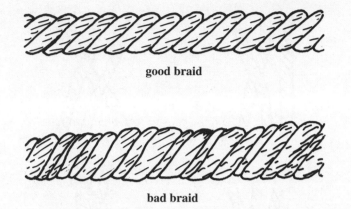

good braid

bad braid

A properly spun two-strand braid will have even tension throughout.

significantly compromise that point. Splicing is simply adding line to one side. Make sure to have plenty of overlap between the preceding line and the new one and to use line of similar diameter.

- To prevent the line from unraveling, finish the free end with an overhand knot.

If you are in a hurry—needing a piece of short line right then—there is a quicker alternative:

- Using spun cord, grab one end between the thumb and forefinger of your left hand and roll it in one direction—on the thigh—with your right palm.
- Repeat this process until the whole line is done and is tight.
- Continue holding the line in your left hand and grasp the other end with your right hand.
- Place the middle between your teeth and move your hands so that you have both ends tightly held in one hand.
- Release the line from your mouth. Due to the tension created from rolling the line on your leg, the two strands will spin together.

THREE-STRAND BRAID
A three-strand braid is ideal for making straps and belts. Use the following guidelines to make a three-strand braid:

Three-strand braid.

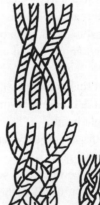

Four-strand braid.

- Tie the three lines together at one end and lay the lines out so that they are side by side.
- Pass the right-side strand over the middle strand.
- Pass the left-side strand over the newly formed middle strand.
- Repeat this process, alternating from side to side (right over middle; left over middle), until done.
- To prevent the line from unraveling, tie the end.

FOUR-STRAND BRAID

A four-strand braid is ideal for use as a rope. It provides the strength and shape desired and is far superior for this purpose to either the two-strand or three-strand braids. To make a four-strand braid, follow these directions:

- Tie the four lines together at one end and lay the lines out so that they arc side by side.
- Pass the right-hand strand over the strand immediately to its left.
- Pass the left-hand strand under the strand directly to its right and over the original right-hand strand.
- Pass the new outside right strand over the strand immediately to its left.
- Pass the new outside left strand under and over the next two strands, respectively, moving to the right.
- Repeat this process (right strand over strand immediately to its left; left strand under and over the two strands immediately to its right).
- Splice as needed.

KNOTS

SQUARE KNOT

A square knot is used to connect two ropes that have an equal diameter.

Square knot.

DOUBLE SHEET BEND

A double sheet bend is used to connect two ropes of differing diameter.

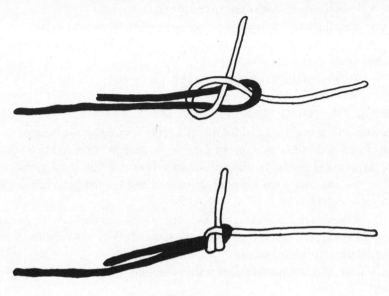

Double sheet bend.

OVERHAND FIXED LOOP

A fixed loop has multiple uses in a survival setting. The biggest problem with using this knot is getting it undone. If this is a concern, use a bowline instead.

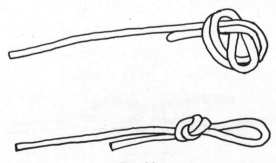

Fixed loop.

BOWLINE

A bowline is a fixed loop that is much easier to untie. For this reason, I opt to use it the majority of the time.

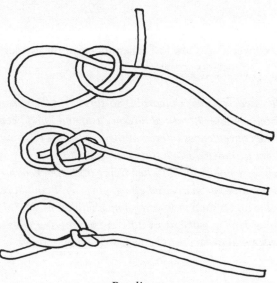

Bowline.

DOUBLE HALF HITCH

A double half hitch is often used to begin a lashing or just to secure one end of line to a stationary object.

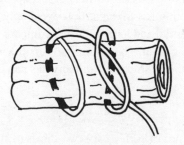

Double half hitch.

13

Glue and Soap

Some basic conveniences are lost when living in the wilderness—or are they?

> *After nearly a year of learning to survive in the various global climates I realized how accustomed I had become to the conveniences offered at the local store. Although Elmer's glue and Dove soap were nice luxuries to have, they were not available when living in the backcountry. With a little ingenuity and effort, however, I could create a glue and a soap that weren't much different. The glue allowed me to make many different improvised tools and the soap allowed me to be welcome again at home.*

IMPROVISED GLUES

ANIMAL GLUE
The effectiveness of animal glue depends on how well it is made, the cleanliness of the wood's surface, and whether you size the wood before applying the glue. Once the wood is cleaned, sizing will help fill the wood's gaps and seal its surface. To clean the material's surface of all oils and debris, use either the lye mixture (discussed earlier) or a soap like Fels-Naptha with warm water and a toothbrush. Sizing is done by simply applying a first coating of glue to the material and letting it dry. I compare this process to using primer before applying paint. The primer protects the wall, providing a better surface for the paint to stick to. Animal glues can be made from sinew, hide, and hide scrapings.

Sinew Glue
Fill a large pot (or a no. 10 coffee can) two-thirds of the way full of sinew, cover it with water, and bring to a boil for 2 to 3 hours. During this time,

stir occasionally and remove any debris that floats to the top. Add water if it looks like the sinew may burn. Next, pour the light syrup (perhaps a little runnier then Elmer's glue) through a fine porous cloth onto a wide tray. Ideally it will be between ¼ to ½ inch thick. Set it in a cool area that provides a breeze (or use a fan) and let it dry. Once it has dried, cut or break it into smaller pieces and store it in a cool dry place that is protected from animals, rodents, and insects.

If you need to use the glue at that moment, just keep it warm. If working with wood or fibers keep it around 140 degrees; if you're working with sinew or other animal parts keep the glue at about 120 degrees. No matter what, don't let it get above 180 degrees. At that high temperature the glue loses a lot of its adhesive qualities. If dried, the glue will need to be reconstituted before using. To do this, place a piece of the glue in a pot, cover with water, and wait several hours until it plumps up. Heat it to around 160 degrees—stirring occasionally—until it reaches a uniform consistency. Lower the temperature of the syrup until it reaches the temperature desired for its use.

Hide Glue
The best material for hide glue is obtained from the scrapings created during the tanning process (membraning). If you don't have scrapings, the hide itself can actually be used with or without hair. If you decide to use the hide, however, it's best to clean it of fat and hair first. To turn hide scrapings into glue use the same steps as you did when making glue from sinew except boil it for approximately 1 hour. Pour the thickened syrup through a porous material. Wring the moisture out of the hide and into the same container. If the hide provides a lot of moisture, you may need to boil the liquid for a short time to return it to its syrupy consistency. At this point the temperature can be reduced based on the work you intend to do or the glue can be dried in the same fashion as done with sinew.

FISH GLUE
The skin and air bladder of fish can be made into fairly effective glue. When using skin, remove all meat, fat, and scales and wash it thoroughly. Next, cut it into strips and prepare it in the same way that you would sinew or rawhide. The biggest difference is that fish glue will not totally dry. In fact, at best you'll end up with a medium-thick syrup as your final product.

PITCH GLUE

Pitch glue is most often made from pine, fir, or spruce, each of which tends to bleed the pitch outside its bark. To make it, try to gather as much pure pitch as you can (dirt will compromise the quality). The hard pitch can be easily placed into a container and wet pitch can be removed with a knife and then scraped into your container. Since pitch becomes brittle if over-cooked and it needs to be used when warm, only prepare small amounts at a time (enough for the intended task). Heat the pitch until it turns into a liquid—removing debris as it becomes obvious. If you don't have a container to heat the pitch in, use a dry nonporous rock strategically placed next to the fire. Pitch may flame up if placed too close to the fire, so be careful! Adding powdered eggshells to the liquid pitch will make the glue stronger and more flexible. To use, apply the wet pitch to the object in the same fashion you would any other glue.

SOAP

Soap is more than just a nice convenience. It also helps us clean wounds, clothes, eating utensils, and cooking gear.

PLANT SOAP

There are many plants that have cleansing properties. Most contain a lather-producing substance called saponin. Saponins work by making foam when they are mixed with water and the foam lifts off dirt and grease. The most common of these plants include:

Name	Plant Part
Soapwort (bouncing bet)	Whole plant
Soapbark	Inner bark
Soapberry	Fruit
Soaproot	Bulb
Acacia	Pods
Yucca	Root

To create lathery suds from most soap plants simply crush the plant part, add moisture, and rub it between your hands. To save the plant part for later use, just let it dry.

LYE SOAP MADE USING WOOD ASH

To make soap the old-fashioned way you'll need white ash, water (rain or springwater is best since it won't contain any undesirable minerals), animal fat (grease), plant oil (optional), salt (optional), a wooden container (plastic or stainless steel can also be used), and a wooden stirring stick. Before making the soap itself, you'll need to make lye water and prepare your animal fat.

Making Lye Water

To create this alkaline solution (lye water), mix approximately 2 gallons of hardwood white ash with 1 gallon of water (2:1 ratio) and stir them together. Be sure to use a wooden barrel, plastic bucket, or stainless steel container and to stir with a wooden stick. Do not use aluminum or tin containers since they are badly corroded by the caustic solution. Let sit for several hours and then pour the solution through a porous cloth into another container. Be sure to wear rubber gloves, eye protection, and an apron to protect your clothes. To determine if the mixture is right, place an egg or small potato in the solution (make sure it has enough room to float in the liquid—even if you have to lean the bucket to one side). If it sinks, the solution is too weak; if it floats and turns sideways, it is too strong. When the mixture is just right, the egg will float so that approximately ½ to 1 inch of its top is showing above the surface. If the egg sinks, you can boil the lye water down—making it stronger—until it supports the egg correctly. If the egg turns sideways, you can add water (1 cup at a time)—making it weaker—until it supports the egg correctly. CAUTION: THIS SOLUTION CAN AND WILL BURN YOUR SKIN AND YOUR EYES AND IS HARMFUL IF SWALLOWED. THE CONTAINER SHOULD BE COVERED, MARKED, AND KEPT OUT OF ANIMALS' AND CHILDREN'S REACH. If any of the lye solution gets on your skin, wash it off with vinegar. If it gets in your eyes, rinse thoroughly for 20 minutes and seek immediate medical attention.

Preparing the Animal Fat

The fat of most animals can be used for making soap. Remove the fat from the meat, cut it into small cubes, place it in a cast-iron frying pan, and melt it slowly over a low heat source. As a general rule, 1 pound produces about 1 cup of grease. Once melted, pour the grease through a porous cloth. To further clean the grease, mix it with equal amounts of water and bring it to a boil. Next, remove it from the heat and add ¼ cup of cold water and let it cool. Once the fat has hardened, scrape away anything that looks dirty. Since the hardened fat is sitting on the water, it is best to remove it to a dry container until ready for use. This final product can be put aside for several weeks before using but if this is done be sure to store it in a cool area that is away from animals, rodents, and insects. If you don't want to use animal fat, use any oils that can also be used for cooking.

Making Soap

You will need three containers (remember, no tin or aluminum) and the largest of the three should be twice as big as the others. To determine how much fat and lye you'll need figure on using a ratio of 12 pounds grease (approximately 30 cups) to 20 gallons of lye water. If you only want a small batch, simply adjust the ratio accordingly (for example: 1 pound of grease to 1.66 gallons of lye water or .6 pounds of grease to 1 gallon of lye water). Using the two smaller containers, heat up the appropriate amount of fat and lye water. To prevent the grease from burning, add ½ inch of water to the pot. Once the grease has melted, spoon it into the larger heated pot and then add the lye water. For large batches use two people and transfer small equal amounts of grease and lye water (stirring as you go) until done. Be sure to keep heating the mixture throughout the whole process.

To determine if the mixture is right use the following rule of thumb:
• If a thick film of grease forms on top, you need more lye.
• If the mixture doesn't thicken, you need more grease.

Once the mixture has a creamy, light caramel appearance you can test it to determine if it is done. Place a small amount of the soap on a glass or china plate and let it cool. When cool, if done, it will appear transparent with white streaks and specks throughout. If it is gray and weak looking or has a gray outer margin, it needs more lye. If it cools with a gray skin over it, it needs more fat. If done, you can store the liquid soap in a wooden container and use as needed.

If you want bar soap, you'll need to reduce the soap's water content. Adding a handful of salt will separate the soap and water. Once the salt is added, let the mixture cool. During this time the soap will separate from the water and will float on top of it. Remove the soap, add a small amount of water, heat to a boil for a few minutes, let it cool, and then skim the soap off the top again. At this point you can rewarm the soap and pour it into your awaiting molds to dry (this can be something as simple as a glass cake pan). If you are using a wooden container, soak it overnight in water and then line it with a wet cloth before pouring the soap in. Other containers should be greased (don't use tin or aluminum). Cover the soap and let it dry overnight. Once dry, remove the soap and use a wire cutter to cut it into useful sizes. At this point the soap is still green and needs to air dry for at least one month. Stack it so that it gets good air circulation in an area that is free from sunlight and moisture.

14

Primitive Navigation

Convenience stores provide travelers with an opportunity to get directions. Unfortunately, they are not available in the wilderness.

On the third day of my first navigation trip it seemed like we had been walking forever when we finally hit an old logging road. Saplings were sprouting everywhere on the road; it was obvious that no one had been on it for a long time. As a group we looked at our maps and yelled with joy when it appeared to be the road we were looking for. This meant we were less than a ½ mile from our final point. We began following it toward our destination, enjoying the rest that the much easier route provided. Or so we thought. Two hours later we gave in to the rapidly approaching darkness and made camp. The next day we triangulated and were saddened to see we had taken the wrong road and that we were farther away from our final destination than when we had started the previous day. That day I realized how powerful the skills of navigation were. Man-made features could be so deceiving. When we finally reached our point, the ache in my muscles provided the motivation needed to learn as much as I could about navigation.

USING A STICK AND SHADOW

Using a flat level area, clear away all debris until a 3-foot circle of dirt is all that remains. Sharpen both ends of a straight stick and then push one end into the ground until the stick's shadow falls onto the center of the cleared area. Mark the shadow tip with a twig (or other appropriate material). Wait approximately 10 minutes and place another twig at the shadow tip's new location. Draw a straight line between the two markers and then another line perpendicular to it. Since the sun rises in the east and sets in the west, the first marking on the shadow line is west and the second one is east.

In the Northern Hemisphere the sun will be south of your location and in the Southern Hemisphere the sun's side will be north of you. This is not always true, however, and—depending on where you are—the stick and shadow may not even be an option for use. The following guidelines will help you decide when to use a stick and shadow to determine your cardinal directions:

• For a stick and shadow method to be reliable it cannot be used at greater than 66.6 degrees north and south latitude.

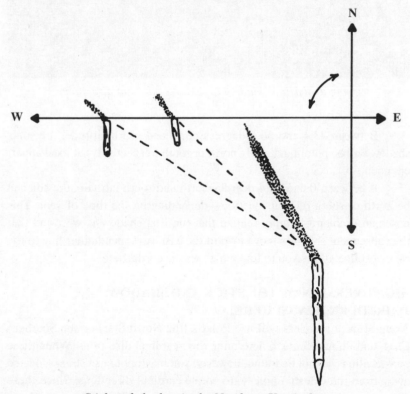

Stick and shadow in the Northern Hemisphere.

Using a stick and shadow to find our cardinal directions.

• Between 23.4 and 66.6 degrees north and south latitude, the sun's shadow will be pointing directly north or south (respectively) at local apparent noon.

• If between 0 and 23.4 degrees north and south latitude, the sun can be north or south of your location—depending on the time of year. This poses no problem—simply realize that the first shadow is west and that the subsequent shadows move toward the east. A perpendicular line to the east/west line allows you to find which way is north/south.

NIGHT VERSION OF THE STICK AND SHADOW (NORTHERN HEMISPHERE)

At night most travelers will use Polaris (the North Star) or the Southern Cross and Pointer Stars to determine their cardinal directions. When these constellations cannot be found, however, you may opt to use stars—located away from the celestial poles—to create cardinal directions. Since these stars generally move from east to west they can provide the same east/west line as shown with the stick and shadow.

Find a straight 5-foot stick and push it into the ground at a slight angle. Next, tie a piece of line to the top of the stick ensuring that it is long enough to reach the ground with lots to spare. Lying on your back, position yourself so that you can pull the cord tautly and hold it next to your temple. Move your body around until the taut line is pointing directly at the selected, non-circumpolar star or planet. At this point, the parachute cord represents the star's shadow. Place a rock at the place where the line touches the ground and repeat the process every 10 minutes or so. Similar to the stick and shadow, the first mark is west and the second one is east. A perpendicular line will aid you in determining north and south.

If you plan to travel at night, you should find and use a sturdy 7-foot-long walking stick. When walking, keep the stick in front of you to protect your face from branches and to ensure that the ground is there.

NAVIGATING WITH A WATCH

NORTHERN HEMISPHERE
Point the watch's hour hand toward the sun and holding it in this position, draw an imaginary line between the hour hand and 12:00 (1:00 if

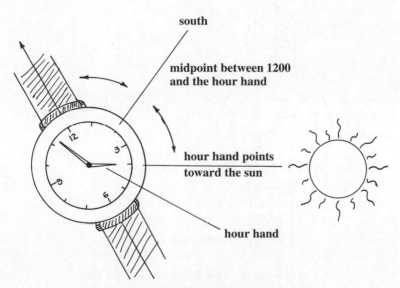

Using a watch in the Northern Hemisphere.

daylight saving time). This imaginary line represents a southern heading. Draw another line perpendicular to this one to determine N/S/E/W.

SOUTHERN HEMISPHERE

In the Southern Hemisphere, point the watch's 12:00 symbol (1:00 if daylight saving time) toward the sun and holding the watch in this position, draw an imaginary line midway between the 12:00 symbol and the hour hand. This imaginary line provides an approximate northern heading. Another line drawn perpendicular to the original one makes it possible to determine N/S/E/W.

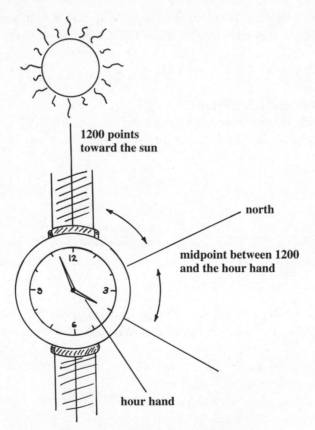

1200 points toward the sun

north

midpoint between 1200 and the hour hand

hour hand

Using a watch in the Southern Hemisphere.

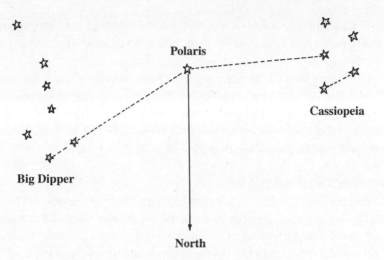

Finding Polaris using the Big Dipper and Cassiopeia.

CONSTELLATIONS

NORTHERN HEMISPHERE
In the Northern Hemisphere, Cassiopeia or the Big Dipper is a very useful tool for helping you find Polaris—the North Star. The Big Dipper looks like a cup with a long handle. Cassiopeia is made up of five stars that form a large W with its opening facing the Big Dipper. During a 24-hour period, the Big Dipper and Cassiopeia will do a complete rotation around Polaris. Halfway between these constellations, Polaris (the North Star) can be found. It is located at the very end of the Little Dipper's handle. Contrary to popular belief, it is not the brightest star in the sky, but instead, it is dull and uninviting. It is always within 1 degree of true north at any given time of the year.

When both constellations cannot be seen, you can still find your cardinal directions by doing the following:

• Big Dipper: at the forward tip of the Big Dipper, there are two stars. Extend a line approximately four to five lengths beyond the second star to find Polaris.

- Cassiopeia: from the center of Cassiopeia, extend out a line approximately four to five times the distance, between any two of its stars, to find Polaris.
- Orion: Orion the hunter circles the earth directly above the equator. The leading star of Orion's Belt (called Mintaka) rises exactly due east and sets exactly due west. The belt is formed by three close stars in line at the center of the figure. When Orion is not directly on the horizon, its east-west path makes it ideal for use with a night stick and shadow.

SOUTHERN HEMISPHERE

To find the cardinal directions in the Southern Hemisphere, use the Southern Cross (four stars forming a cross) and the Pointer Stars. A False Cross looks similar to the Southern Cross and it may present a problem. The False Cross is less bright than the Southern Cross and its stars are more widely spaced. In fact, the southern and eastern arms of the actual Southern Cross are two of the brightest stars in the sky. The Pointer Stars are simply two stars—side by side—in close proximity to the Southern Cross.

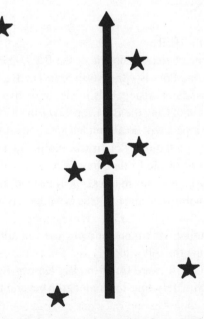

Orion's Belt rises in the east and sets in the west.

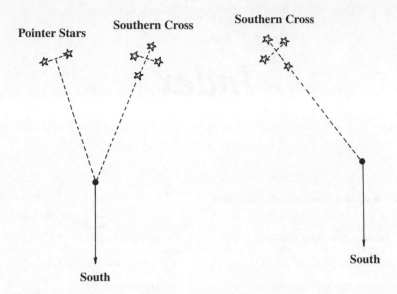

Finding a southern heading using the Southern Cross and Pointer Stars.

To establish a southern heading, extend an imaginary line (from the top toward the bottom) out of the bottom of the cross. Draw another imaginary line perpendicular to the center of the Pointer Stars. At the point where the lines intersect, draw a third line straight down toward the ground—this line represents a southern direction.

USING A MAGNETIZED NEEDLE

A magnetized needle will provide a north-south line when allowed to float freely on water. Since you probably won't have a magnet with you in the woods, you will need to magnetize the needle prior to your journey. If this seems impractical, then either magnetize your knife before leaving or bring a small piece of silk along for the trip. By rubbing the needle across the magnetized knife or silk, it will become magnetized and will function as does the north-seeking arrow of a compass. Find a stump or similar item with standing water in the center. Place a leaf—or other material that will float freely—in the water. Next set the needle on the floating leaf and wait. It may take up to 2 minutes for the leaf to stop moving—and when it does— the needle should indicate a north-south direction.

Index